NEW DIRECTIONS FOR INSTITUTIONAL RESEARCH

J. Fredericks Volkwein, *Penn State University*
EDITOR-IN-CHIEF

Larry H. Litten, *Dartmouth College*
ASSOCIATE EDITOR

Understanding the College Choice of Disadvantaged Students

Alberto F. Cabrera
Pennsylvania State University

Steven M. La Nasa
Pennsylvania State University

EDITORS

Number 107, Fall 2000

JOSSEY-BASS PUBLISHERS
San Francisco

UNDERSTANDING THE COLLEGE CHOICE OF DISADVANTAGED STUDENTS
Alberto F. Cabrera, Steven M. La Nasa (eds.)
New Directions for Institutional Research, no. 107
Volume XXVII, Number 3
J. Fredericks Volkwein, Editor-in-Chief

New Directions for Institutional Research is indexed in *College Student Personnel Abstracts, Contents Pages in Education,* and *Current Index to Journals in Education* (ERIC).

Microfilm copies of issues and chapters are available in 16mm and 35mm, as well as microfiche in 105mm, through University Microfilms Inc., 300 North Zeeb Road, Ann Arbor, Michigan 48106-1346.

ISSN 0271-0579   ISBN 0-7879-5439-X

NEW DIRECTIONS FOR INSTITUTIONAL RESEARCH is part of The Jossey-Bass Higher and Adult Education Series and is published quarterly by Jossey-Bass Inc., Publishers, 350 Sansome Street, San Francisco, California 94104-1342 (publication number USPS 098-830). Periodicals postage paid at San Francisco, California, and at additional mailing offices. POSTMASTER: Send address changes to New Directions for Institutional Research, Jossey-Bass Inc., Publishers, 350 Sansome Street, San Francisco, California 94104-1342.

SUBSCRIPTIONS cost $56.00 for individuals and $99.00 for institutions, agencies, and libraries.

EDITORIAL CORRESPONDENCE should be sent to J. Fredericks Volkwein, Center for the Study of Higher Education, Penn State University, 403 South Allen Street, Suite 104, University Park, PA 16801-5252.

Photograph of the library by Michael Graves at San Juan Capistrano by Chad Slattery © 1984. All rights reserved.

www.josseybass.com

Printed in the United States of America on acid-free recycled paper containing 100 percent recovered waste paper, of which at least 20 percent is postconsumer waste.

CONTENTS

fine Book
8547 - esp Ch 6
A412

EDITORS' NOTES

This volume examines the college-choice decision and gives special attention to underrepresented students. *New Directions for Institutional Research* 107 is published in collaboration with the Association for Institutional Research (AIR) and the Center for the Study of Higher Education at Penn State. The majority of the chapters in this volume are either based on research funded by AIR grants or were presented as papers at a recent Penn State Symposium to celebrate the thirtieth anniversary of the Center for the Study of Higher Education. All the chapters reflect the latest research on the topic by a collection of national scholars.

Improving college participation among minorities and socioeconomically disadvantaged students has dominated much of the federal and state policies in higher education for over three decades (McPherson and Shapiro, 1998). Some of these policies seek to assist talented but socioeconomically disadvantaged and at-risk youth by providing them and their families with information and different types of assistance (Trent, 1992). Others seek to eliminate inability to pay for college by providing various forms of financial assistance ranging from loans and grants to work-study subsidies. Despite an annual investment of over $60 billion on such programs as Chapter I, Talent Search, Gaining Early Awareness and Readiness for Undergraduate Programs (GEARUP), and Financial Aid (College Board, 1999), college participation rates among low-income students and minorities remain disproportionately low (Wilds, 2000; McPherson and Shapiro, 1998; King, 1996).

It stands to reason that one way to improve intervention strategies is having an intimate knowledge of how disadvantaged and at-risk students and their families make decisions about college. This volume of *New Directions for Institutional Research* seeks to address this need by summarizing the latest research on how disadvantaged students develop aspirations toward college, secure college-related qualifications, obtain information about institutions, choose a particular institution over another, and enroll. This volume substantially relies on one of the most comprehensive databases (NCES, 1996), which tracks a representative sample of students from the eighth grade until college enrollment. The analyses reported here, ranging from simple descriptive statistics to logistic regression analyses, are all framed to be accessible to the institutional researchers and the policy audiences they serve. The volume is organized into seven chapters.

In Chapter One, Alberto F. Cabrera and Steven M. La Nasa review the literature on college choice while stressing those few findings pertaining to disadvantaged students. They also advance a workable model seeking to explain the process that students and their families undergo when making decisions about college.

Chapters Two and Three address the college-choice process for low–socioeconomic status (SES) students. Chapter Two reveals the three major tasks that middle school students in general and socioeconomically disadvantaged students in particular must complete on their way to college. It documents college destinations by academic qualifications and high school graduation patterns. Chapter Three examines the role of family- and high school–based variables on the probability of securing college qualifications, completing high school, and applying to college among socioeconomically disadvantaged students. Findings suggest viable intervention strategies aimed at school- and family-based approaches.

In Chapter Four, Susan P. Choy, Laura J. Horn, Lutz Berkner, Anne-Marie Nuñez, and Xianglei Chen, of MPR Associates, discuss at-risk and first-generation college students. Their work integrates more than five years of successful study of how this student population overcomes obstacles to college access.

Chapter Five focuses attention on racial and ethnic differences in college enrollment decisions. Laura W. Perna summarizes and presents original research findings on the influential factors underlying African American and Hispanic decisions to enroll in college.

In Chapter Six, Watson Scott Swail examines in detail the programmatic efforts geared towards making college a reality among disadvantaged U.S. youth. The weakness and strengths of TRIO, Upper Bound, and GEARUP are discussed in terms of political realities and the challenges posed by the need to coordinate several organizations. Having weighed the pros and cons of each program in terms of the research findings, the author formulates four criteria that successful intervention strategies must meet.

Finally, Chapter Seven presents valuable background information on the National Educational Longitudinal Study of 1988, which is the basis for much of this volume. In this chapter, Lutz Berkner provides interested researchers with a roadmap to unlock the power of this important national dataset. Institutional researchers seeking to explore national trends will find this an excellent resource.

Maintaining a vibrant and diversified student body presupposes that the institution has the ability to implement strategies for attracting and retaining diverse students (Clagget, 1992). These effective institutional strategies, in turn, presume a deep understanding of how students choose to attend college. As noted in the 1999 AIR call for research grant proposals, institutions have lacked resources to develop the capacity to create, access, and utilize detailed information about prospective students. This volume enhances this knowledge by advancing workable models that can greatly assist administrators as they seek to assess, develop, and modify institutional enrollment management polices. Knowing what factors are most relevant when a prospective student makes a decision to attend college allows institutions to map out the key data elements involved. This map can then constitute the backbone of a comprehensive enrollment management information system.

Alberto F. Cabrera
Steven M. La Nasa
Editors

References

Clagett, C. "Enrollment Management." In M. A. Whiteley, J. D. Porter, and R. Fenske (eds.), *The Primer for Institutional Research*. No. 7. Tallahassee, Fla.: Association for Institutional Research, 1992.

College Board. *Trends in Student Aid: 1999*. New York: The College Board, 1999.

King, J. E. *The Decision to Go to College: Attitudes and Experiences Associated with College Attendance Among Low-Income Students*. Washington, D.C.: The College Board, 1996.

McPherson, M. S., and Schapiro, M. O. *The Student Aid Game: Meeting Need and Rewarding Talent in American Higher Education*. Princeton, N.J.: Princeton University Press, 1998.

National Center for Education Statistics (NCES). National Educational Longitudinal Study of 1988. Restricted file. Washington, D.C.: National Center for Education Statistics, U.S. Department of Education, 1996. (NCES 96–130)

Trent, W. T. *Measuring Program Impact: What Impacts Are Important to Assess, and What Impacts Are Possible to Measure? A Proposal for Research*. Washington, D.C.: Design Conference for the Evaluation of Talent Search, Office of Policy and Planning, U.S. Department of Education, 1992.

Wilds, D. J. *Minorities in Higher Education: Seventeenth Annual Status Report*. Washington, D.C.: American Council on Education, 2000.

1

This chapter summarizes what we have learned regarding the process that students and their families undergo when making decisions about college. It also presents a comprehensive model synthesizing this literature.

Understanding the College-Choice Process

Alberto F. Cabrera, Steven M. La Nasa

The literature suggests that decisions to go to college are the result of a three-stage process that begins as early as the seventh grade and ends when the high school graduate enrolls at an institution of higher education (Hossler, Braxton, and Coopersmith, 1989). In undergoing each phase of the college-choice process, high school students develop predispositions to attend college, search for general information about college, and make choices leading them to enroll at a given institution of higher education.

Each college-choice phase seems to be associated with a specific age cohort, corresponding to grades seven through twelve (Nora and Cabrera, 1992). Each of these three stages has particular cognitive and affective outcomes that cumulatively prepare high school students to make certain decisions regarding their college education (see Table 1.1).

The literature also suggests that these three stages interact with one another, each affecting the others in subtle and complex ways (Alexander and Eckland, 1975; Sewell and Shah, 1968; Sewell, Haller, and Portes, 1969). Figure 1.1 offers a schematic representation of the process linking the three college-choice stages. Parental encouragement, a pivotal force in the emergence of occupational and educational aspirations, is conditioned by the ability and high school preparation of the child, parental and sibling educational attainment, and access to information about college and costs.

Support for this literature review came from the College Board (contract no. 412–13 CB Low Income Students, 24450) and the Association for Institutional Research (contract no. 99–114–0). The opinions here do not necessarily reflect the opinions or policies of either funding organization, and no official endorsement should be inferred.

Table 1.1. College-Choice Process: Stages, Factors, and Outcomes

Stages	Factors	Outcomes
Predispositions: Grades 7–9	Parental encouragement and support Parental saving for college Socioeconomic status Parental collegiate experiences High school academic resources Student ability Information about college	Reading, writing, math, and critical thinking skills Career and occupational aspirations Educational aspirations Enrollment in college-bound curriculum
Search: Grades 10–12	Parental encouragement and support Educational aspirations Occupational aspirations Socioeconomic status Saliency of potential institutions Student ability High school academic resources	Listing of tentative institutions Narrowing list of tentative institutions Securing information on institutions
Choice: Grades 11–12	Educational aspirations Occupational aspirations Socioeconomic status Student ability Parental encouragement Perceived institutional attributes (quality, campus life, majors, availability, distance) Perceived ability to pay (perceived resources, perceived costs)	Awareness of college expenses and financial aid Awareness of institutional attributes and admission standards Attaining scholastic aptitudes and attitudes Perceived support from family and friends Institutional commitment Submission of applications Preregistration Attendance Application for financial aid

Source: Adapted from Nora and Cabrera, 1992.

Parental encouragement, the availability of information about college, and perceived cost-benefit analysis of attending college also shape the institution set that the student and family will seriously consider (see, for example, McDonough, 1997). In turn, the final decision depends on the saliency of institutions; parental encouragement; financial considerations; the student's high school academic resources; the student's educational and occupational aspirations; and, of course, the student's academic abilities.

Predispositions

The predisposition stage involves the development of occupational and educational aspirations as well as the emergence of intentions to continue education beyond the secondary level. Planning for college begins as early

Figure 1.1. College-Choice Process

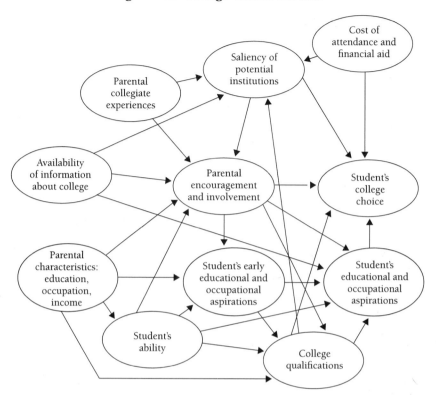

Source: Based on Berkner and Chavez, 1997; Flint, 1993, 1997; Horn, 1997; Hossler and Vesper, 1993; Hossler, Schmit, and Vesper, 1999; Perna, 2000; Sewell and Hauser, 1975; Stage and Hossler, 1989; St. John, 1990; Terenzini, Cabrera, and Bernal, forthcoming.

as the eighth grade, and by the ninth grade most students have already developed occupational and educational aspirations (Eckstrom, 1985; Stage and Hossler, 1989).[1] During this period, junior high school students come to value a particular occupation and begin to see attending college as crucial in securing their occupational goals. Early college plans seem to play the role of a trigger mechanism in securing critical cultural capital. It enables eighth graders and their parents to plan for college-track curriculum and extracurricular activities, to maintain good academic performance, and to secure information about ways to finance college (see, for example, Hossler, Schmit, and Vesper, 1999; McDonough, 1997)

Planning for college is affected by many factors that interact among themselves in a complex manner (Alexander and Eckland, 1975; Sewell and Shah, 1968; Sewell, Haller, and Portes, 1969). Among the factors predicting students' early educational plans, parental encouragement is the strongest (Conklin and Dailey, 1981; Hossler, Schmit, and Vesper, 1999; Stage and Hossler, 1989).

Parental encouragement has two dimensions. The first is motivational: parents maintain high educational expectations for their children. The second is proactive: parents become involved in school matters, discuss college plans with their children, and save for college (Flint, 1992, 1993; Henderson and Berla, 1994; Hossler and Vesper, 1993; Hossler, Schmit and Vesper, 1999; Miller, 1997; Perna, 2000; Stage and Hossler, 1989).

Development and maintenance of postsecondary education aspirations among high school students is proportionally related to the frequency and consistency with which parents provide encouragement (Flint, 1992). Conklin and Daily (1981), for instance, have found that high school graduates entering a four-year college were more likely to report consistent parental encouragement from ninth grade through the twelfth grade. In contrast, students entering two-year institutions were more prone to report mixed parental support across the high school years.

College destinations are also related to parental involvement in school activities. Perna (2000) has demonstrated that parental involvement in school activities, as early as junior high, predicts whether the student will enroll in a four-year college or university upon high school graduation.

Saving for college is presumed to be an objective and key expression of parental encouragement to pursue a college degree (Stage and Hossler, 1989; Hossler and Vesper, 1993). Flint (1992, 1993) argues that this encouragement manifests itself when parents initiate college savings plans, advise their children on a range of acceptable college costs, and search for additional sources of financial support. The extent of parental belief in education and the foundation for parental involvement can be found in a 1996 Gallup Poll of parents of college-bound high school students. The poll shows that the vast majority of parents (92 percent) regard a college education as the most important investment they can make for their children (Miller, 1997).

The amount of saving for college is associated with parents' own socioeconomic status. Miller (1997) notes that two-thirds of low-income parents surveyed in her study had saved little—10 percent or less of the total college educational costs. She has also found that most low-income parents expect to finance college education through financial aid. Reliance on financial aid varied in direct proportion with family income. Low-income parents were more likely to expect to go into debt to finance their children's college education than were upper-income parents (65 percent versus 40 percent).

In addition to socioeconomic status, parental saving seems to be conditioned by parents' own knowledge of college costs and ways to finance a college education (Flint, 1991, 1992, 1993; Miller, 1997). Hossler and Vesper (1993) report that the parents of Indiana eighth graders are more prone to save when they are cognizant of college costs. Although little research exists on parental knowledge of costs and student college choice, some research indicates that knowledge of college costs and preparation to finance college education are more prevalent among upper-income parents (see, for example, Miller, 1997; McDonough, 1997; Olson and Rosenfeld, 1984). In view of the role of information on parental propensity to save, Hossler, Schmit, and Vesper (1999) recommend providing parents with periodic financial information, especially during the early high school grades. Hossler and Vesper (1993) suggest that information need not be detailed; general information may suffice to motivate parents to acquire enough knowledge to start saving for their children's postsecondary education.

The ability of the student seems to moderate the amount and quality of parental encouragement. Research on occupational attainment indicates that parents provide the most encouragement to the child with the highest academic ability (Hossler, Braxton, and Coopersmith, 1989).

Search

The search stage involves the accumulation and assimilation of information necessary to develop the student's short list of institutions. This choice set, often heavily influenced by parental encouragement (Conklin and Dailey, 1981; Flint, 1992; Hossler, Braxton, and Coopersmith, 1989; Litten, 1982), consists of a group of institutions that the student wants to consider and learn more about before making a matriculation decision. This stage usually begins during tenth grade and ends by the middle of twelfth grade (Hossler, Braxton, and Coopersmith, 1989). At this stage, students begin to interact actively with potential institutions (Attinasi, 1989). Visiting campuses, securing catalogues, and talking to friends about college are some of the activities used in seeking such information (Hossler, Braxton, and Coopersmith, 1989; Litten, 1982).

The choice set is largely dependent on the level of sophistication and thoroughness of the search process. This degree of sophistication appears to be determined by socioeconomic factors (McDonough, 1997; Olson and Rosenfeld, 1984). In general, more affluent students, compared with their less-well-off peers, tend to rely on several sources of information (including private counselors to guide the process), are more knowledgeable of college costs, are more likely to broaden the search to include a wider geographical range, tend to consider higher-quality institutions, and have parents who planned and saved for college expenses (Flint, 1992, 1993; Hamrick and Hossler, 1996; Horn and Chen, 1998; Hossler, Schmit, and Vesper, 1999; Hossler, Schmit, and Bouse, 1991; Hossler and Vesper, 1993; Leslie, Johnson, and Carlson, 1977; McDonough, 1997; McDonough, Antonio, Walpole, and Perez, 1998; Miller, 1997; Olivas, 1985; Tierney, 1980).

Saliency of Potential Institutions. Prior to applying to college, students develop strong preferences among institutions, evaluate their own qualifications for admission, ponder alternative mechanisms for financing college, and apply to colleges (Berkner and Chavez, 1997; Choy and Ottinger, 1998; Hossler, Braxton, and Coopersmith, 1989). Development of expectations and perceptions about the quality of the institution, campus life, availability of majors, and one's ability to finance enrollment are the primary considerations shaping actual matriculation (Choy and Ottinger, 1998; Hossler, Schmit, and Vesper, 1999; McDonough, 1997; Tinto, 1993). High school seniors develop mental pictures of the institutions under consideration (St. John, Paulsen, and Starkey, 1996). These images lead the high school senior to form predispositions and commitments toward certain institutions. Within this context, perceptions of the availability of financial aid not only positively influence thoughts of matriculation but also predispose students to select a particular institution (Choy and Ottinger, 1998; Hossler, Schmit, and Vesper, 1999; Jackson, 1978; Olson and Rosenfeld, 1984; King, 1996; St. John, 1994a, 1994b; St. John, Paulsen, and Starkey, 1996). Moreover, Flint (1993) has found that knowledge of financial aid allows parents to consider a wider range of institutions than they might otherwise.

Students' Access to Information. For three decades, socioeconomic factors also have mediated students' access to information about college. Using data from the National Longitudinal Study of the High School Class of 1972, Tierney (1980) has reported that low–socioeconomic status (SES) students had fewer information sources than upper-level SES students did. Leslie, Johnson, and Carlson (1977) report similar findings. These researchers have found low-SES students relying on high school counselors as the single most likely source of information about college. In contrast, upper-income students report a variety of sources including parents, students, catalogues, college representatives, and private guidance counselors. Although low-income students may be limited in their access to a variety of sources of information, availability of high school–based academic information resources seems to level the playing field.

Financial Aid and the Role of Parents: Knowledge and Intergenerational Effects. Knowledge of financial aid also influences the strategies parents follow when devising financial plans for their children (Flint, 1993). Based on the Parent Survey of the 1980 Senior Class of High School and Beyond, Olson and Rosenfeld (1984) have found that college-educated parents are more knowledgeable than low-income parents not only about the different types of financial aid programs available but about qualification criteria as well. Net of a parents' gender and college expectations for the child, parents' education and having children in college exerted the strongest effects on parental knowledge of financial aid programs. Strategies followed in securing information also affect the amount of knowledge the parents have regarding avenues to finance their children's college education. Olson and Rosenfeld report that parents' knowledge of financial aid increases the most when they employ a variety of information-seeking strategies, including consulting with high school guidance counselors and bank loan officers as well as reading a variety of college financing pamphlets and books. Ikenberry and Hartle (1998) have found that the amount and quality of information on college financing varies proportionally with socioeconomic status. Overall, upper-income families are more knowledgeable.

How active parents are in planning to finance their children's college education also seems to be dependent upon their own collegiate financial experiences. Drawing from the 1990 National Postsecondary Student Aid Study, Flint (1997) documented an intergenerational effect whereby parents' plans to finance their children's' college education were shaped by the strategies parents themselves followed when financing their own undergraduate educations. Having been recipients of parental financial support or financial aid themselves motivated parents to contemplate a wide range of possibilities to finance their children's college education.

The Role of High School Counselors on Low-Income Students' Postsecondary Plans. King (1996) noted that low-income high school seniors who constantly consulted with a high school counselor regarding postsecondary plans were more disposed to plan attending college. The same effect on postsecondary plans was noted among those low-income students who received information about admissions and financial aid from representatives of colleges' admission and financial aid offices. Meeting college qualifications also seems to motivate low-income high school students to search for information about college at higher rates than those exhibited by equally qualified upper-income peers. Using data from the High School Class of 1992 (NELS:88), Berkner and Chavez (1997) found college qualified low-income students more likely to discuss financial aid with high school counselors and teachers (72%) and college representatives (49%) than were their middle-income (63% and 45%) and high-income (47% and 34%) peers.

Students' Perceptions of Ability to Pay. Students' perceptions of their and their family's ability to pay also appear to weigh heavily in college selection among low-income students. Leslie, Johnson, and Carlson (1977) have found low-income students weighting financial assistance more heavily than do upper-income students when narrowing the list of potential institutions of higher education. This finding seems to be indirectly supported by Tierney (1980), who notes that low-income seniors' probability of attending college is heavily influenced by the perceived availability of financial assistance.

Search and Success in College. The importance of securing accurate information about college extends well beyond decisions to enroll in college. Satisfaction with college and achieving educational and career goals appears to be conditioned largely by the quality of information secured in high school (see, for example, Hossler, Schmit, and Vesper, 1999; Hossler and Vesper, 1993). Using a longitudinal sample of Indiana eighth graders, Hamrick and Hossler (1996), for instance, have found high satisfaction levels with collegiate experiences and certainty of college major among those college students who relied on a wide variety of sources of information while making decisions about college during their high school years.

Choice

Applying to college and actually enrolling have been scrutinized under two lenses: one is economic in nature, and the other is sociological (St. John, Paulsen, and Starkey, 1996). The economic perspective regards enrollment as the result of a rational process in which an individual estimates the economic and social benefits of attending college, comparing them with those of competing alternatives (Manski and Wise, 1983). The sociological approach examines the extent to which high school graduates' socioeconomic characteristics and academic preparation predispose them to enroll at a particular type of college and to aspire to a particular level of postsecondary educational attainment. As noted by St. John, Paulsen, and Starkey (1996), both approaches converge in portraying low-income students as sensitive to financial considerations and academic preparation for college.

Tuition and Enrollment. The economic approach to the study of the college-choice process has dominated the evaluation of the effects of public policy seeking to expand and equalize student access to college (St. John, 1994b). Underlying the significant investment in financial aid lies the assumption that ability to pay plays an important role in students' decisions about college (Jackson, 1978, 1988; Manski and Wise, 1983; St. John, 1994a, 1994b).

Research consistently shows a significant and negative relationship between tuition increases and enrollment, an empirical relationship that conforms to public perceptions. Leslie and Brinkman (1988) have reviewed twenty-five studies examining the connection between tuition and college enrollment by type (two-year and four-year) and control (public and private). They have found all students to be sensitive to tuition costs.[2] Leslie and Brinkman (1988) have estimated that every $100 increase (in 1982–1983 dollars) would reduce enrollments between 1.8 and 2.4 percentage points. In his review of ten tuition enrollment studies published between 1975 and 1996, Heller (1997) has found a pattern consistent with that identified by Leslie and Brinkman. Taking into account the differences in methodologies used, data sets employed, period of time under consideration, and type of students and institutions examined, Heller (1997) concludes that every tuition increase of $100 dollars leads to a decline in enrollment from 0.5 to 1.00 percentage points.

Tuition, Student Aid, and Low-Income Students. Low-income students' decisions to attend college appear to be highly sensitive to tuition and financial aid levels (Heller, 1997; Hossler, Hu, and Schmit, 1998; St. John, 1994b). Several recent studies suggest that the increasing cost of attendance has compelled low-income students to restrict their enrollment to less expensive institutions (McPherson and Schapiro, 1998; St. John, 1994b). In summarizing their extensive research on the effect of net cost increases (college expenses minus resources) on enrollment, McPherson and Schapiro estimate that a $150 net cost increase (in 1993–1994 dollars) will result in a 1.6 percentage point decline in enrollment among low-income students.

Although low-income students can be adversely affected by tuition increases, financial aid can positively predispose them to attend college (Berkner and Chavez, 1997). Using data from the National Longitudinal Study of the High School Class of 1972, Jackson (1978) has found that low-SES students are more likely to apply to college when offered financial assistance. Manski and Wise (1983) have calculated that 17 percent fewer low-income students would have attended college in the 1979–80 academic year had it not been for the Basic Educational Opportunity Grants program.

Noting that economic research had not taken into account the role of different types of financial aid when estimating the effect of tuition, St. John (1990) has examined the joint effect of price and subsidies on enrollment decisions among college applicants from the 1982 High School and Beyond Study (sophomore cohort). Table 1.2 summarizes St. John's estimates for the whole cohort and by income levels, based on $1,000 increases in either tuition or financial aid.[3] He finds all college applicants to be sensitive to both tuition and financial aid (see Table 1.2, column 2). Controlling for student socioeconomic background and high school grades, tested ability, and curricular track, a $1,000 (in 1982–1983 dollars) increase in tuition would depress total enrollment by about 3 percentage points (see column 2 in Table 1.2). St. John also finds federal financial aid policy to be effective in increasing enrollment: college applicants are more sensitive to financial aid than they are to changes in tuition when making decisions to attend college. For instance, a $1,000 increase in grants, loans, and work-study programs would yield increases in enrollment ranging from 4 to 5 percentage points (see column 2 in Table 1.2). Noticeable differences in the effect of tuition and aid have been observed when college applicants are examined by income quartiles. As a whole, low-income students have been found to be highly responsive to grants and unresponsive to loans and work-study programs (see column 3 in Table 1.2). Although slightly more sensitive to tuition increases than the average applicant, a low-income student is almost three times more likely to respond positively to increases in grants than to increases in tuition. A $1,000 increase in grants has been found to boost enrollment rates among low-income college students for about 9 percentage points; an equivalent increase in tuition would depress enrollment among low-income student for about 3.4 percentage points.[4] The literature, with some exceptions (for example, Hansen, 1983), provides empirical support for the current policy of targeting grants to low-income students.

College Destinations. Examination of the college destinations of students from different economic backgrounds has led to conflicting findings regarding the extent to which the present financial aid system provides equal educational opportunities in college choice. Although McPherson and Schapiro (1998) find evidence of an inequitable college-choice system in which a student's family income conditions college destinations, Alexander, Pallas, and Holupka (1987) and Hearn (1988, 1991) provide evidence of a meritocratic system in which socioeconomic factors play a secondary role to such factors as academic ability, preparation for college, and educational expectations. At the core of these discrepancies lie the level of analysis and the type of controls these studies employ.

At the aggregate level, evidence seems to support the notion of inequity of educational opportunities. McPherson and Schapiro (1998) use the American Freshman Surveys of first-time, full-time college freshmen between 1980 and 1994 to analyze enrollment changes of students of dif-

**Table 1.2. Predicted Percentage-Point Changes in Probabilities
of Enrollment per $1,000 Increase in Tuition or Financial Aid
by College Applicants in the High School Class of 1980**

			Family Income		
Tuition and Financial Aid	All Students	Low (<$15,000)	Low-Middle ($15,000– $24,999)	Middle ($25,000– $39,999)	Upper ($40,000 or >)
Tuition	−2.8**	−3.4**	−3.9**	−3.3**	−1.4**
Grants	4.3**	8.8**	3.5*	3.1*	4.1
Loans	3.8**	1.1	5.3**	6.3**	3.6
Work study	4.6**	5.1	3.1	NA	NA

Note: *$p < .05$; **$p < .01$; NA = not applicable.
Source: Adapted from St. John, 1990.

ferent income levels. As shown in Figure 1.2, they have identified a pattern
of "increasing stratification of public higher education by income" (p. 48).
Most 1994 lower-income freshmen (81 percent) enrolled at public institutions and clustered in community colleges at rates disproportionally higher
(50 percent) than those exhibited in the upper-income (17 percent) and
highest-income (12 percent) levels. Although 41 percent of the upper-
income and 47 percent of the richest students enrolled at a university, only
13.5 percent of the poorest students did so. Contrasting 1994 with 1980,
McPherson and Schapiro find that the proportion of lower-income students
in public two-year institutions increased slightly (46 percent versus 47 percent), although the participation of upper-income and richest students
in the public two-year sector declined at a steadier rate: 17 percent versus
14 percent and 15 percent versus 9 percent, respectively. The pattern of college attendance among middle-income students was mixed. Altogether, this
group showed a slight increase from 16 percent to 17 percent in their enrollment at private four-year institutions and a moderate increase from 20 percent to 25 percent in their participation rates at public four-year institutions.
McPherson and Schapiro find that most of the changes in enrollment rates
among middle-income students resulted from a redistribution of enrollments from the two-year to the four-year sector. They attribute this pattern
of college attendance to increasing college tuition costs in the private sector, which compelled low-income students to opt for less expensive institutions, and to substantial tuition discounts at private institutions aimed at
middle-income students.

Similar to McPherson and Schapiro's study, Berkner and Chavez (1997)
report a direct and positive association between postsecondary destinations
and family income and parental education. However, the pattern of social
stratification that Beckner and Chavez depict is not as accentuated. In examining the role of parental socioeconomic status in postsecondary destina-

**Figure 1.2. 1994 Proportional Enrollment Distribution
by Institution Type Within Income Groups**

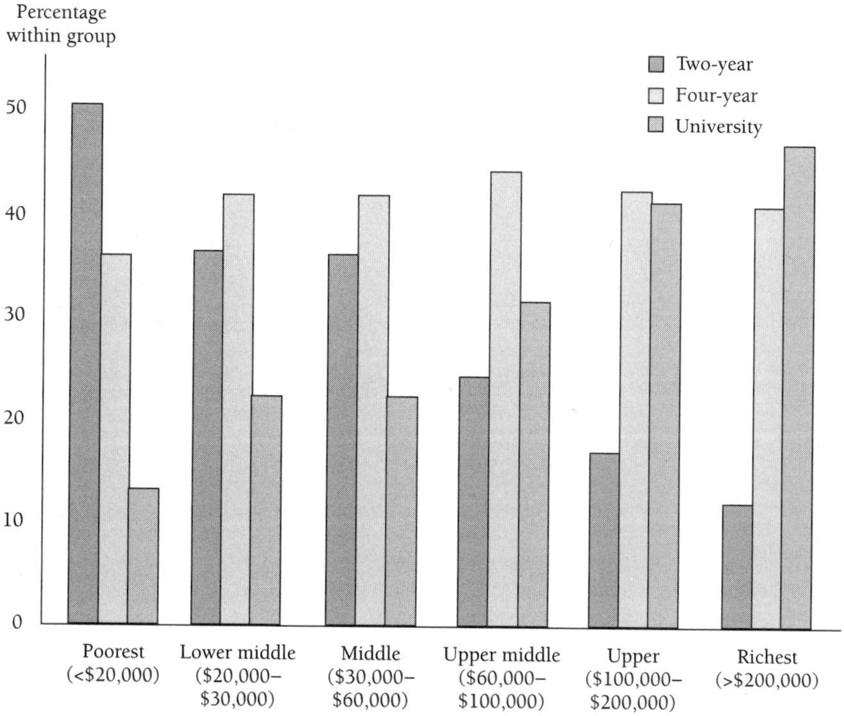

Source: Based on data provided in McPherson and Schapiro, 1998.

tions among a representative sample of the 1992 high school graduation class, Berkner and Chavez have developed a rather creative test: measure the extent to which a high school senior's plans of enrolling at a four-year institution were fulfilled within two years of high school graduation. In terms of family income, 72 percent of low-income seniors materialized their plan. Seventy-seven percent and 89 percent of middle-income and high-income seniors achieved this goal. About 17 percent of low-income students ended up in a two-year institution, although only 7.5 percent of upper-income seniors did so (see Figure 1.3). In terms of parental education (see Figure 1.4), seniors with non-college-educated parents were less likely to fulfill their plans of attending college immediately after high school (65 percent) compared with those whose parents had some college (73 percent) or held a college degree (87 percent).

The dominant role of socioeconomic backgrounds in college destinations appears to diminish when longitudinal data bases, along with powerful statistical models that control for socioeconomic background, preparation

Figure 1.3. 1994 Percentage Enrollment Distribution of 1992 High School Graduates Who Planned to Attend a Four-Year Institution Immediately After High School by 1998 Parental Income

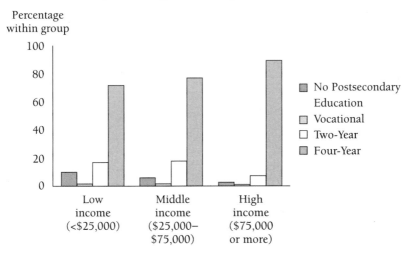

Source: Based on Table 10 in Berkner and Chavez, 1997, p. 19.

for college, and college application behaviors, are brought to bear (for example, Baker and Vélez, 1996). In a series of logistic regression models aimed at examining enrollment decisions at either two- or four-year institutions, Alexander, Pallas, and Holupka (1987) have found that academic preparation for college was more important than SES in college destinations among 1972 high school graduates. Along with preparation for college, taking steps to meet college admission requirements has recently been found to play a key role in eliminating differences in college participation rates between low-SES high school graduates and their middle- and upper-SES counterparts. As shown in Figures 1.5 and 1.6, Berkner and Chavez (1997) have found that college-qualified 1992 high school seniors from poor educational and income backgrounds enrolled at four-year institutions at rates comparable to or slightly lower than those of seniors whose families had some college education (76 percent versus 81 percent) or were middle income (83 percent versus 82 percent) provided they took college entrance examinations and submitted applications to four-year institutions.[5] After examining net costs (total cost of college attendance minus student aid) of college attendance for dependent low-income students, Berkner and Chavez conclude that financial aid was responsible for removing ability to pay as a deterrent for these otherwise college-qualified individuals.

Socioeconomic status does not appear to be a major constraint for attending private or selective institutions as long as the low-SES high school graduate meets college qualifications criteria (Berkner and Chavez, 1997;

Figure 1.4. 1994 Percentage Enrollment Distribution of 1992 High School Graduates Who Planned to Attend a Four-Year Institution Immediately After High School by Parental Education

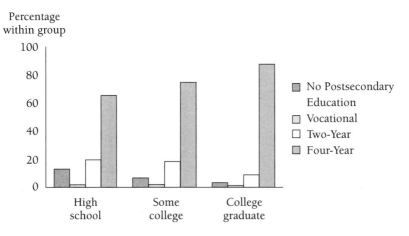

Source: Based on Table 10 in Berkner and Chavez, 1997, p. 19.

Hearn, 1988, 1991). Using data from the 1980 High School and Beyond Study, Hearn finds that the direct effect of family income in attending higher cost institutions diminishes once precollege academic variables are taken into account. He reports enrollment at high-cost institutions to be influenced the most by educational expectations along with high school grades, curricular track, and academic ability. He concludes that the small size of the direct income effect might have been attributable to the growth of financial aid programs in the 1970s, which facilitated enrollment at high-cost institutions among academically able low- and middle-income high school graduates. In terms of attending selective institutions, Hearn (1991), again, finds that precollege preparation played a key role among 1980 high school graduates. Although finding academic factors dominating college destinations, Hearn also reports SES exerting an indirect small influence in the selectivity of the institutions that African Americans attended. Among this group, "students with less educated or lower-income parents . . . were especially likely to attend lower-selectivity institutions even if their academic ability and achievements were high" (p. 164).

Taken as a whole, then, the literature on college choice depicts decisions to go to college as the by-product of a three-stage process, which begins as early as the seventh grade, if not earlier, and ends when the student enrolls in a postsecondary institution. In this process, parents, middle schools, high schools, and a student's characteristics are key to developing plans and aspirations toward college, securing the necessary qualifications, applying to college, and enrolling. The next two chapters examine how this process takes

Figure 1.5. 1994 Percentage Enrollment Distribution of College-Qualified 1992 High School Graduates Who Took an Entrance Examination or Applied for Admission to a Four-Year Institution by Income

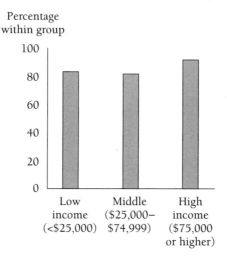

Source: Based on Table 23 in Berkner and Chavez, 1997, p. 43.

Figure 1.6. 1994 Percentage Enrollment Distribution of College-Qualified 1992 High School Graduates Who Took an Entrance Examination or Applied for Admission to a Four-Year Institution by Parental Education

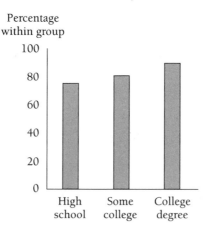

Source: Based on Table 23 in Berkner and Chavez, 1997, p. 43.

place among socioeconomically disadvantaged students. Chapter Two depicts the path followed by poor eighth graders on their path to college, whereas Chapter Three pinpoints those factors facilitating the path to college. Both chapters rely on analyses conducted on the National Educational Longitudinal Study of 1988 (NCES, 1996), which follows a representative sample of 1988 eighth graders through the college-choice process.

Notes

1. Eckstrom (1985) has found that 61 percent of those high school graduates who enrolled in college had made the decision to go to college by ninth grade.

2. To facilitate comparisons across studies, Leslie and Brinkman (1988) have standardized tuition elasticities. The standardized measure, termed Student Price Response Coefficient (SPRC), represents the change in probability of enrollment due to a $100 change in tuition prices. SPRCs can be converted to tuition elasticities by multiplying them by a factor of 3, assuming that one-third of the college-age population attends college (see Leslie and Brinkman, 1987; St. John, 1994a).

3. St. John's probabilities of enrollment are based on $100 dollar increases in either financial aid or tuition. Heller (1997) has shown that these elasticities could be better framed in $1,000 increments.

4. St. John (1990) advances several explanations to account for the fact that his elasticities are lower than previous estimates. Unlike previous studies, St. John's has included financial aid in the computation of tuition elasticities; this method reduces cost of attending, dampening the effect of tuition. Moreover, he has included far more controls in the form of high school preparation and motivation to pursue postsecondary education than did previous research. In contrast to McPherson and Schapiro (1998), who rely on time series analyses, St. John examines the effects of tuition and financial aid following a cross-sectional design. Finally, he suggests that tuition elasticities might have changed over time, reflecting changes in policies, costs, and targeting of student aid.

5. The odds of college enrollment clearly favored seniors from high socioeconomic backgrounds. College participation rates for those college-qualified high school seniors whose parents were college educated or had high incomes were 93.5 percent and 91.8 percent, respectively.

References

Alexander, K. L., and Eckland, B. K. "Basic Attainment Processes: A Replication and Extension." *Sociology of Education,* 1975, *48*(4), 457–495.

Alexander, K. L., Pallas, A. M., and Holupka, S. "Consistency and Change in Educational Stratification: Recent Trends Regarding Social Background and College Access." *Research in Social Stratification and Mobility,*1987, *6,* 161–185.

Attinasi, L. C. "Getting In: Mexican Americans' Perceptions of University Attendance and the Implications for the Freshman Year Persistence." *Journal of Higher Education,* 1989, *60*(3), 247–277.

Baker, T. L., and Vélez, W. "Access to and Opportunity in Postsecondary Education in the United States: A Review." *Sociology of Education,* 1996, extra issue, 82–101.

Berkner, L., and Chavez, L. *Access to Postsecondary Education for the 1992 High School Graduates.* Washington, D.C.: National Center for Education Statistics, U.S. Department of Education, U.S. Government Printing Office, 1997. (NCES 98–105)

Choy, S. P., and Ottinger, C. *Choosing a Postsecondary Institution.* Statistical Analysis Report. Washington, D.C.: Office of Educational Research and Improvement, National Center for Education Statistics, U.S. Department of Education, 1998. (NCES 98–080)

Conklin, M. E., and Dailey, A. R. "Does Consistency of Parental Educational Encouragement Matter for Secondary Students?" *Sociology of Education*, 1981, *54*(4), 254–262.

Eckstrom, R. B. *A Descriptive Study of Public High School Guidance: Report to the Commissions for the Study of Precollegiate Guidance and Counseling.* Princeton, N.J.: Educational Testing Service, 1985.

Flint, T. A. "Does Financial Aid Make Students Consider Colleges with a Wider Cost Range?" *Journal of Student Financial Aid*, 1991, *21*(2), 21–32.

Flint, T. A. "Parental and Planning Influences on the Formation of Student College Choice Sets." *Research in Higher Education*, 1992, *33*(6), 689–708.

Flint, T. A. "Early Awareness of College Financial Aid: Does It Expand Choice?" *Review of Higher Education*, 1993, *16*(3), 309–327.

Flint, T. A. "Intergenerational Effects of Paying for College." *Research in Higher Education*, 1997 *38*(3), 313–344.

Hamrick, F. A., and Hossler, D. "Diverse Information-Gathering Methods in Postsecondary Decision-Making Process." *Review of Higher Education*, 1996, *19*(2), 179–198.

Hansen, W. L. "The Impact of Student Financial Aid on Access." In J. Froomkin (ed.), *The Crisis in Higher Education.* New York: Academy of Political Science, 1983.

Hearn, J. C. "Attendance at Higher-Cost Colleges: Ascribed, Socioeconomic, and Academic Influences on Student Enrollment Patterns." *Economics of Education Review*, 1988, *7*(1), 65–76.

Hearn, J. C. "Academic and Nonacademic Influences on the College Destinations of 1980 High School Graduates." *Sociology of Education*, 1991, *64*(3), 158–171.

Heller, D. E. "Student Price Response in Higher Education: An Update to Leslie and Brinkman." *Journal of Higher Education*, 1997, *68*(6), 624–659.

Henderson, A. T., and Berla, N. *A New Generation of Evidence: The Family Is Critical on Student Achievement.* Washington, D.C.: National Committee for Citizens in Education, 1994.

Horn, L. *Confronting the Odds: Students At Risk and the Pipeline to Higher Education.* Washington, D.C.: National Center for Education Statistics, U.S. Department of Education, U.S. Government Printing Office, 1997. (NCES 98–094)

Horn, L., and Chen, X. *Toward Resiliency: At-Risk Students Who Make It to College.* Washington, D.C.: Office of Educational Research and Improvement, U.S. Department of Education, 1998.

Hossler, D., Braxton, J., and Coopersmith, G. "Understanding Student College Choice." In John C. Smart (ed.), *Higher Education: Handbook of Theory and Research.* Vol. 5. New York: Agathon Press, 1989.

Hossler, D., Hu, S., and Schmit, J. "Predicting Student Sensitivity to Tuition and Financial Aid." Paper presented at the annual meeting of the American Educational Research Association, San Diego, California, April 1998.

Hossler, D., Schmit, J., and Bouse, G. "Family Knowledge of Postsecondary Costs and Financial Aid." *Journal of Financial Aid*, 1991, *21*(1), 4–17.

Hossler, D., Schmit, J., and Vesper, N. *Going to College: How Social, Economic, and Educational Factors Influence the Decisions Students Make.* Baltimore: Johns Hopkins University Press, 1999.

Hossler, D., and Vesper, N. "An Exploratory Study of the Factors Associated with Parental Saving for Postsecondary Education." *Journal of Higher Education*, 1993, *64*(2), 140–165.

Ikenberry, S. O., and Hartle, T. W. *Too Little Knowledge Is a Dangerous Thing: What the Public Thinks and Knows About Paying for College.* Washington, D.C.: American Council on Education, 1998.

Jackson, G. A. "Financial Aid and Student Enrollment." *Journal of Higher Education* 1978, *49*(6), 548–574.

Jackson, G. A. "Did College Choice Change During the Seventies?" *Economics of Education Review*, 1988, *7*(1), 15–28.

King, J. E. *The Decision to Go to College: Attitudes and Experiences Associated with College Attendance Among Low-Income Students.* Washington, D.C.: The College Board, 1996.

Leslie, L. L., and Brinkman, P. T. *The Economic Value of Higher Education.* New York: American Council on Education, Macmillan, 1988.

Leslie, L. L., Johnson, G. P., and Carlson, J. "The Impact of Need-Based Student Aid upon the College Attendance Decision." *Journal of Education Finance,* 1977, 2(3), 269–285.

Litten, L. H. "Different Strokes in the Applicant Pool: Some Refinements in a Model of Student College Choice." *Journal of Higher Education,* 1982, 53(4), 383–401.

Manski, C. F., and Wise, D. A. *College Choice in America.* Cambridge: Harvard University Press, 1983.

McDonough, P. M. *Choosing Colleges: How Social Class and Schools Structure Opportunity.* Albany: State University of New York Press, 1997.

McDonough, P. M., Antonio, A. L., Walpole, M., and Perez, L. X. "College Rankings: Democratized College Knowledge for Whom?" *Research in Higher Education,* 1998, 39(5), 513–538.

McPherson, M. S., and Schapiro, M. O. *The Student Aid Game: Meeting Need and Rewarding Talent in American Higher Education.* Princeton, N.J.: Princeton University Press, 1998.

Miller, E. I. "Parents' Views on the Value of a College Education and How They Will Pay for It." *Journal of Student Financial Aid,* 1997, 27(1), 20.

National Center for Education Statistics (NCES). National Educational Longitudinal Study of 1988. Restricted file. Washington, D.C.: National Center for Education Statistics, U.S. Department of Education, 1996. (NCES 96–130)

Nora, A., and Cabrera, A. F. "Measuring Program Outcomes: What Impacts Are Important to Assess and What Impacts Are Possible to Measure?" Paper prepared for the Design Conference for the Evaluation of Talent Search. Washington, D.C.: Office of Policy and Planning, U.S. Department of Education, 1992.

Olson, L., and Rosenfeld, R. A. "Parents and the Process of Gaining Access to Student Financial Aid." *Journal of Higher Education,* 1984, 55(4), 455–480.

Olivas, M. A. "Financial Aid Packaging Policies: Access and Ideology." *Journal of Higher Education,* 1985, 56(4), 462–475.

Perna, L. W. "Differences in College Enrollment Among African Americans, Hispanics, and Whites." *Journal of Higher Education,* 2000, 71(2), 117–141.

St. John, E. P. "Price Response in Enrollment Decisions: An Analysis of the High School and Beyond Sophomore Cohort." *Research in Higher Education,* 1990, 31(2), 161–176.

St. John, E. P. "Assessing Tuition and Student Aid Strategies: Using Price-Response Measures to Simulate Pricing Alternatives." *Research in Higher Education,* 1994a, 35(3), 301–335.

St. John, E. P. *Prices Productivity, and Investment: Assessing Financial Strategies in Higher Education.* ASHE-ERIC Higher Education Reports, no. 3. Washington, D.C.: ERIC Clearinghouse on Higher Education, George Washington University Press, 1994b.

St. John, E. P., Paulsen, M. B., and Starkey, J. B. "The Nexus Between College Choice and Persistence." *Research in Higher Education,* 1996, 37(2), 175–220.

Sewell, W. H., Haller, A. O., and Portes, A. "The Educational and Early Occupational Attainment Process." *American Sociological Review,* 1969, 34(1), 82–92.

Sewell, W. H., and Hauser, R. M. *Education, Occupation, and Earnings: Achievement in the Early Career.* New York: Academic Press, 1975.

Sewell, W. H., and Shah, V. P. "Social Class, Parental Encouragement, and Educational Aspirations." *American Journal of Sociology,* 1968, 73(5), 559–572.

Stage, F. K., and Hossler, D. "Differences in Family Influences on College Attendance Plans for Male and Female Ninth Graders." *Research in Higher Education,* 1989, 30(3), 301–315.

Terenzini, P. T., Cabrera, A. F., and Bernal, E. M. *Swimming Against the Tide: The Poor in American Higher Education.* Washington, D.C.: The College Board, forthcoming.

Tierney, M, S. "The Impact of Financial Aid on Student Demand for Public/Private Higher Education." *Journal of Higher Education,* 1980, 51(5), 527–545.

Tinto, V. *Leaving College: Rethinking the Causes and Cures of Student Attrition.* Chicago: University of Chicago Press, 1993.

ALBERTO F. CABRERA is associate professor and senior researcher with the Center for the Study of Higher Education at Pennsylvania State University.

STEVEN M. LA NASA is a graduate research assistant and doctoral candidate with the Center for the Study of Higher Education at Pennsylvania State University.

2

Using data from the National Educational Longitudinal Study of 1988, this chapter examines the wide disparity of college-choice activities between socioeconomic groups. In order to highlight this disparity, the authors analyze three tasks that all students must complete on their path to college.

Three Critical Tasks America's Disadvantaged Face on Their Path to College

Alberto F. Cabrera, Steven M. La Nasa

According to estimates by the National Center for Education Statistics, almost three million youths were enrolled at the eighth grade in 1988.[1] Seven hundred thousand of them came from the lowest–socioeconomic status (SES) quartile. This chapter examines the fate of these students as they endure three critical tasks on their path to college: acquiring the necessary academic qualifications for college work, securing a high school diploma, and applying and enrolling in a four-year institution of higher education.

Figure 2.1 depicts the path to college followed by one thousand 1988 eighth graders, regardless of their socioeconomic background. As one examines a student's progression through these three critical checkpoints, we find that the defining characteristic of the college enrollee is the acquisition of college qualifications,[2] which begins as early as the eighth grade.[3] Students who secure college qualifications while in high school have a higher chance of enrolling in college than those who do not. Seventy percent of college-qualified high school graduates enrolled in a four-year institution[4] immediately following high school completion, whereas only 13 percent of those who did not secure college qualifications enrolled. Even obtaining only a minimum level of college qualifications increased a student's likelihood of

Support for this literature review came from the College Board (contract no. 412-13 CB Low Income Students, 24450) and the Association for Institutional Research (contract no. 99-114-0). The opinions here do not necessarily reflect the opinions or policies of either funding organization, and no official endorsement should be inferred.

Figure 2.1. College-Choice Process for 1,000 Eighth-Grade Students, 1988

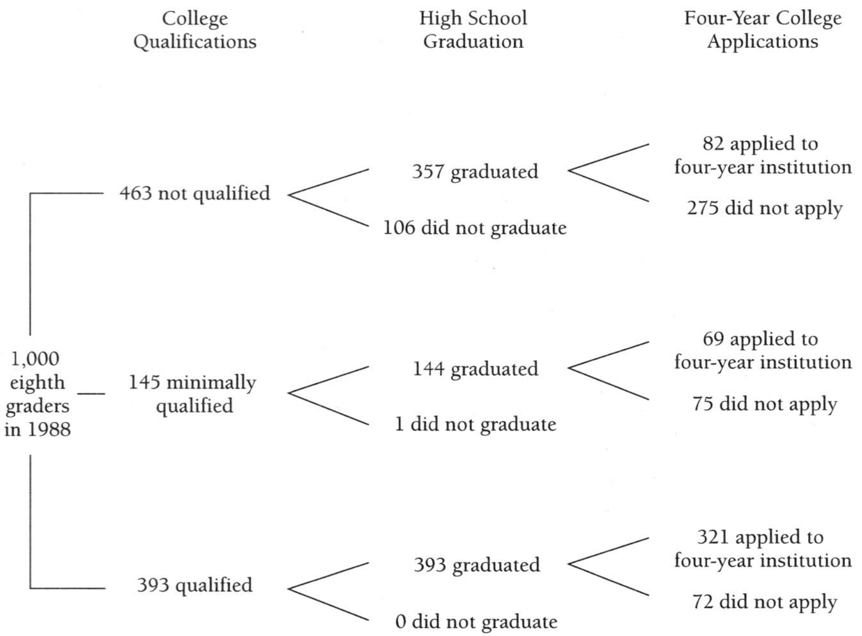

1,000 eighth graders in 1988

College Qualifications → High School Graduation → Four-Year College Applications → Institution Type of First Enrollment

463 not qualified

- 357 graduated
  - 82 applied to four-year institution
  - 275 did not apply
- 106 did not graduate

	None	Vocational	Two-Year	Four-Year
82 applied to four-year institution	13	4	17	48
275 did not apply	175	20	80	0

145 minimally qualified

- 144 graduated
  - 69 applied to four-year institution
  - 75 did not apply
- 1 did not graduate

	None	Vocational	Two-Year	Four-Year
69 applied to four-year institution	6	2	15	46
75 did not apply	35	6	34	0

393 qualified

- 393 graduated
  - 321 applied to four-year institution
  - 72 did not apply
- 0 did not graduate

	None	Vocational	Two-Year	Four-Year
321 applied to four-year institution	11	2	30	278
72 did not apply	22	5	45	0

Source: Based on National Educational Longitudinal Study, 1988 (NCES, 1996).

enrolling in a four-year institution. Thirty-two percent of those high school graduates who secured only minimum college qualifications during high school enrolled in a four-year institution after graduation.

Figure 2.1 also shows the importance of securing college qualifications as an important precondition of high school graduation. Nearly all students securing minimal qualifications and above completed high school, whereas only 77 percent of those students not meeting college qualifications secured a high school diploma.

As important as it is to become college qualified and obtain a high school diploma to enroll in a four-year institution, college attendance can be triggered only when the student actually submits college applications. The application process in itself presents numerous hurdles, which include concerns over college costs, uncertainties in the selection of a major, completion of college applications forms, and filling out extremely complex financial aid forms. Even for the most college-qualified student, the application process may present intimidating challenges. Eighteen percent of those most-qualified high school graduates did not apply to a four-year institution. Regardless of qualifications, if students opt not to apply, they are not eligible to enroll.

College-Choice Variance by Socioeconomic Status

Substantial differences in the patterns of college choice emerge when one takes into account a student's SES. Seventy-one percent of the lowest-SES students (see Figure 2.2) did not obtain the academic qualifications necessary to support college enrollment. Moreover, lowest-SES students were 24.2 percent less likely to be college qualified than the national average (see Figures 2.1 and 2.2). In contrast, only 30.3 percent of the highest-SES students did not obtain the requisite college qualifications (see Figure 2.3). Moreover, 55 percent of the highest-SES students were college qualified by the end of their senior year. Once socioeconomically disadvantaged students overcome the college qualification hurdle, their chances to obtain a high school diploma even out. The graduation rates among the lowest-SES students at least minimally qualified were indistinguishable from the corresponding graduation rates for the highest-SES students (see Figures 2.2 and 2.3).

Completing the third task, actually applying to a four-year institution, appears to be particularly challenging for the lowest-SES students. Only 65.6 percent of the college-qualified high school graduates from lowest-SES backgrounds actually applied to a four-year institution. This rate is 17 percent and 22 percent below the national rate of similarly qualified eighth graders and the rate for students from high-SES backgrounds, respectively.

Once lowest-SES students completed the third task and submitted an application, their chances of enrolling in a four-year institution improved

Figure 2.2. College-Choice Process for 1,000 Low-SES Students

College Qualifications	High School Graduation	Four-Year College Applications	Institution Type of First Enrollment			
			None	Vocational	Two-Year	Four-Year
714 not qualified	477 graduated	70 applied to four-year institution	17	5	10	38
		407 did not apply	288	31	88	0
	237 did not graduate					
134 minimally qualified	132 graduated	46 applied to four-year institution	11	2	6	27
		86 did not apply	46	7	33	0
	2 did not graduate					
151 qualified	151 graduated	99 applied to four-year institution	5	1	13	79
		52 did not apply	23	5	24	0
	0 did not graduate					

1,000 eighth graders in 1988

Source: Based on National Educational Longitudinal Study, 1988 (NCES, 1996).

Figure 2.3. College-Choice Process for 1,000 High-SES Students

College Qualifications | High School Graduation | Four-Year College Applications | Institution Type of First Enrollment

1,000 eighth graders in 1988

303 not qualified
- 268 graduated
  - 89 applied to four-year institution
  - 179 did not apply
- 35 did not graduate

	None	Vocational	Two-Year	Four-Year
89 applied to four-year institution	9	4	19	57
179 did not apply	95	11	73	0

148 minimally qualified
- 147 graduated
  - 85 applied to four-year institution
  - 62 did not apply
- 1 did not graduate

	None	Vocational	Two-Year	Four-Year
85 applied to four-year institution	5	2	17	61
62 did not apply	24	6	32	0

549 qualified
- 548 graduated
  - 478 applied to four-year institution
  - 70 did not apply
- 1 did not graduate

	None	Vocational	Two-Year	Four-Year
478 applied to four-year institution	14	2	38	424
70 did not apply	13	5	52	0

Source: Based on National Educational Longitudinal Study, 1988 (NCES, 1996).

dramatically to the point of closely resembling the national average and the rate for the highest-SES students. Among college-qualified, lowest-SES high school graduates who applied for college, 80 percent enrolled in a four-year institution. College attendance rates for the high-SES and average eighth graders who applied to college were 89 percent and 87 percent, respectively.

The path to college among socioeconomically disadvantaged eighth graders can best be characterized as hazardous. By the twelfth grade, only 285 out of 1,000 eighth graders from lowest-SES backgrounds had secured at least minimal college qualifications. By the end of the senior year, only 215 had applied to four-year colleges or universities. Two years after high school graduation, only 144 had enrolled at a four-year institution. Disadvantaged students' path to college is not only perilous but also unfair. On a national basis, 278 out of 1,000 eighth graders who secured college qualifications, graduated from high school, and applied to a four-year institution enrolled in one (see Figure 2.1). In contrast, only 79 low-SES students who met the same three conditions enrolled in a four-year institution. Compared with equally college-qualified high school graduates from upper-SES backgrounds, a lowest-SES high school graduate was 22 percent less likely to apply to college (see Figures 2.2 and 2.3).

Chapter Three examines those factors that enable all high students to complete each task. It pays particular attention to those factors that facilitate success for each task among socioeconomically disadvantaged students by examining the role of ability, the amount and quality of parental encouragement and involvement received, early educational and occupational aspirations, the amount of information available about college, and acquisition of college qualifications.

Notes

1. This estimate is based on the National Longitudinal Study of 1988 (NCES, 1996). This database is formed of a series of surveys conducted on a nationally representative sample of 1988 eighth graders (see Chapter Seven).

2. Developed by Berkner and Chavez (1997), the college qualification index approximates college admissions criteria by collapsing cumulative academic course grade point average, senior-class rank, aptitude test scores, and the SAT and ACT scores. Adjustments were made to account for the nature of a student's academic program. Berkner and Chavez have found that just meeting minimal college qualifications significantly predicts college enrollment. For the purpose of this essay, the college-qualified categories of somewhat qualified, very qualified, and highly qualified were collapsed into the category of qualified.

3. Figures 2.1, 2.2, and 2.3 are based on panel weight (F3PNLWT), which estimated the U.S. population of eighth graders to be 2,968,427 in 1988. Of them, only 89.9 percent (2,668,022) had valid information in the college qualification index. Subjects with missing values for high school completion and four-year applications have also been excluded from analysis.

4. College enrollment was ascertained using F3SEC2A1, an index developed by Berkner and Chavez (1997) to track the first type of institution attended as of 1994.

References

Berkner, L., and Chavez, L. *Access to Postsecondary Education for the 1992 High School Graduates.* Washington, D.C.: National Center for Education Statistics, U.S. Department of Education, U.S. Government Printing Office, 1997. (NCES 98–105)

National Center for Education Statistics (NCES). *National Educational Longitudinal Study of 1988.* Restricted file. Washington, D.C.: National Center for Education Statistics, U.S. Department of Education, 1996. (NCES 96–130)

ALBERTO F. CABRERA *is associate professor and senior researcher with the Center for the Study of Higher Education at Pennsylvania State University.*

STEVEN M. LA NASA *is a graduate research assistant and doctoral candidate with the Center for the Study of Higher Education at Pennsylvania State University.*

3

Using data from the National Educational Longitudinal
Study of 1988, this chapter seeks to gain a better
understanding of what factors assist economically
and sociologically underprivileged Americans to ready
themselves for college.

Overcoming the Tasks on the Path to College for America's Disadvantaged

Alberto F. Cabrera, Steven M. La Nasa

Enrolling in a four-year college requires the completion of at least three critical tasks: meeting minimal college qualifications, graduating from high school, and actually applying to a four-year college or university (see Chapter Two). Eighty-three percent of those 1988 eighth graders who completed these three tasks enrolled in college (based on Figure 2.1). As compared with the track taken by average and upper-socioeconomic status (SES)–originated eighth graders, the path to college among low-SES students is extraordinary difficult. Examining data on 1,000 eighth graders, we found that only 144 enrolled in college immediately after high school graduation (based on Figure 2.2). A number of points may shed light on the characteristics and backgrounds of lowest-SES students that place them at a disadvantage. Those pertain to family income, parental education, gender, ethnicity, and exposure to at-risk factors.

Who Is a Low-SES Eighth Grader?

Nearly one-third of students located in the lowest-SES quartile reported family incomes in the middle or high categories. As evinced by Table 3.1, income is a strong but not absolute predictor of SES status, however ($r = .425$). Also relevant is the lack of association between race and SES quartile. The low correlation between ethnicity and SES ($r = .183$) indicates

Support for this literature review came from the College Board (contract no. 412–13 CB Low Income Students, 24450) and the Association for Institutional Research (contract no. 99–114–0). The opinions here do not necessarily reflect the opinions or policies of either funding organization, and no official endorsement should be inferred.

that race is not a good proxy for a student's SES, a finding consistent with those of Bernal, Cabrera, and Terenzini (2000). Gender does not play an important role in the prediction of status either.

Parental level of education, more so than income, however, does begin to address characteristics more central to an understanding of the issues that lowest-SES students face throughout their college-choice process. After all, college education is a cultural asset critical in social mobility (McDonough, 1997). Using a sample of 1995 low-income high school students who took the SAT, King (1996) notes that low-income high school seniors who reported planning to attend college at higher rates than expected had parents familiar with higher education. When considering those parents with at least some exposure to the requirements of college and the college-choice process, our results indicate that at most 23 percent of lowest-SES parents can provide their children with any guidance based on firsthand collegiate experiences (see Table 3.1). In contrast, nearly all of highest-SES students (99.3 percent) grew up in families knowledgeable of postsecondary education.

Parental education is not, however, the only differential factor that is affecting lowest-SES students on the path to college. Lowest-SES students also tend to be differentially at risk. Chen and Kaufman (1997) have found that the likelihood of dropping out of high school is in direct proportion to the extent

Table 3.1. Income, Parental Education, Gender, and Ethnicity by SES Quartile of Eighth Graders in 1988

| | | SES | | | | |
		Lowest (Percentage)	Middle Lowest (Percentage)	Middle Upper (Percentage)	Highest (Percentage)	Degree of Association (R)
Income	Low	70.5	36.7	21.0	5.9	
	Middle	25.3	57.6	68.4	55.0	.425
	High	4.2	5.7	10.6	39.2	
Parents' highest education	HS or less	77.0	38.3	9.7	0.7	
	Some college	22.5	58.7	71.0	16.4	.655
	College graduate	0.5	3.0	19.3	82.9	
Gender	Male	47.7	49.5	50.6	52.4	.034
	Female	52.3	50.5	49.4	47.6	
Ethnicity	Asian/Pacific Islander	2.4	2.8	3.5	5.1	
	Hispanic	22.1	9.8	6.1	3.9	.183
	African American	22.7	14.3	10.9	6.8	
	Native American	2.5	1.5	1.4	0.4	
	White	51.2	71.6	78.1	83.6	

Note: Estimates are based on the National Educational Longitudinal Study of 1988 (NCES, 1996) panel weight (F3PNLWT).

the student has (1) a record of poor academic performance during junior high school, (2) a history of high school dropouts in the family, (3) been held back a grade, (4) been raised by a single parent, and (5) changed schools more than twice. These five risk factors tend to be associated with lowest-SES students more so than students from other SES groups (see Table 3.2).

The degree of association for three of Chen and Kaufman's risk factors and SES is fairly high and warrants attention. Lowest-SES students were 35 percent more likely to receive lower grades during the sixth through the eighth grades than were their high-SES counterparts. This period may be critically important, as this is the point where powerful predispositions toward college attendance are formed. Furthermore, this is the time when students lay the academic foundation upon which other subject matter is built during high school. Failure to achieve adequate academic preparations, even at this early stage, may inhibit a student's future prospects.

Additionally, lowest-SES students were almost 23 percent more likely to have older siblings that had opted to not complete high school. This characteristic may be extremely damaging to a student's prospects because first-hand knowledge of dropping out may increase acceptance of this path as a viable alternative. Finally, lowest-SES students tended to be held back one grade more often that their higher-SES peers. Only 9 percent of high-SES students were held back a grade, whereas 30 percent of lowest-SES students were held back at least once during their academic career. Not only do each of these five risk factors tend to affect lowest-SES students more when the factors are considered individually, but when examining the risk factors as a group, they are also more prevalent among the lowest-SES students.

Table 3.2. Risk Factors by SES Quartile

	SES				
	Lowest (Percentage)	Middle Lowest (Percentage)	Middle Upper (Percentage)	Highest (Percentage)	Degree of Association (R)
Student averaged C's (2.5) or less in grades 6–8	53.4	41.9	33.5	18.5	.267
Student has other siblings who dropped out of high school	27.0	16.1	12.5	4.1	.232
Student was held back a grade	30.7	18.5	13.8	9.0	.210
Student from a single-parent family	33.1	21.1	18.2	12.9	.181
Student changed schools more than twice	33.8	30.3	29.2	28.3	.045

Note: Estimates are based on the National Educational Longitudinal Study of 1988 (NCES, 1996) panel weight (F3PNLWT).

The frequency with which eighth graders experienced at-risk factors correlates negatively with their SES ($r = -.294$). The higher a student's SES, the less likely the student is to be influenced adversely by the presence of risk factors (see Figure 3.1).

On average, lowest-SES students tended to have at least one risk factor influencing their high school performance, whereas the upper-middle- and highest-SES students had less than one factor exerting an influence on their chance of success. This difference, though small, is withstanding. Chen and Kaufman (1997) have shown that an increase in just one more risk factor could increase the likelihood of dropping out of high school.

What Matters?

Thus far, this chapter highlights the vast discrepancies between backgrounds and experiences of the lowest- and highest-SES students on the path to college. Our findings and the supporting college-choice literature suggest that the three tasks listed at the beginning of this chapter (and discussed in depth in Chapter Two) are critical to college enrollment. Evidence shows a clear disparity between the lowest- and highest-SES students with respect to the successful completion of these tasks. To explain the factors that encourage students to complete each task, we have advanced a college-choice model portraying college enrollment as the culmination of a process beginning as early as the eighth grade and ending when the high school graduate submits college applications (see Figure 1.1). In this model, a student's college choice is unavoidably linked to a student's academic ability, the amount and quality of parental encouragement and involvement received, his or her early educational and occupational aspirations, the amount information available about college, and his or her acquisition of college qualifications.

In testing this model, we were limited by the availability of variables in the National Educational Longitudinal Survey of 1988 (NELS) file (NCES, 1996). Nevertheless, the richness of this data enabled our analysis to test most of the propositions embedded into our college-choice model. Because many of the college-choice variables examined are intertwined, we used logistic regression[1] to single out the net effects of individual variables at each step on the path to college. The steps examined by our analysis were (1) acquisition of college qualifications, (2) graduation from high school, and (3) applying to a four-year college or university.

Acquisition of College Qualifications. In following the 1,000 eighth graders in 1988 from lowest-SES backgrounds on the path to college, only 285, less than one-third, secured some degree of college qualifications by the end of their senior year (see Figure 2.2). Of them, 151 were fully college qualified. One hundred and thirty-four obtained minimal college qualifications. In contrast, 697, or over two-thirds, of a similar group of 1,000 upper-SES students secured some degree of college qualifications by their

Figure 3.1. Mean At-Risk Factors Across SES Quartiles

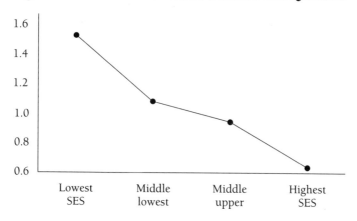

senior year. The majority (549 out of 697) were qualified to begin collegiate work (see Figure 2.2).

King (1996) notes that parental encouragement was a decisive factor in formulating postsecondary plans among a sample of 1995 low-income high school students. Low-income seniors, unsure whether their fathers were pleased with their postsecondary plans, were less likely than their better-off peers within their cohort to aspire to attend a public four-year college or university. King also concludes that income has a pervasive effect on post-secondary plans. The percentage of low-income students planning to attend a four-year institution or college lagged behind those for middle- and upper-income seniors (66 percent versus 80 percent and 85 percent, respectively).

Our results regarding the connection between SES and early post-secondary plans are consistent with King's findings. Lowest-SES eighth graders were 34.5 percent, 25.7 percent, and 13.6 percent less likely to develop postsecondary plans than their upper-, middle-upper-, and middle-lowest-SES counterparts (see Figure 3.2).

Parental involvement in eighth graders' school activities varies in direct relation with SES ($r = .252$). On average, upper-SES students reported higher levels of parental involvement than their lower-SES counterparts (see Figure 3.3).

Research on occupational attainment also indicates that parents provide the most encouragement to the child with the highest academic ability (Hossler, Braxton, and Coopersmith, 1989). Ability does correlate with SES among eighth graders ($r = .442$). Our results also show that lowest-SES eighth graders displayed lower standardized scores in math and reading (see Figure 3.4). And, consistent with the extant literature, we find a significant relationship between parental involvement and a student's ability. However, this correlation is weak ($r = .169$).

Securing at least minimal college qualifications correlates with SES ($r = .377$). Lowest-SES students were 51 percent, 30 percent, and 18 percent

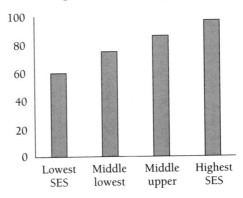

**Figure 3.2. Percentage of Eighth Graders
Planning to Attend College by SES**

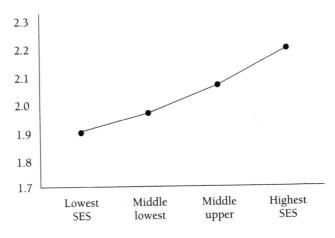

**Figure 3.3. Average Parental Involvement
in School Activities Across SES Quartiles**

less likely to secure minimal college qualifications than their upper, middle-upper, and middle-lowest counterparts, respectively (see actual probabilities in Figure 3.5).

These vast SES gaps narrow substantially once such influential college-choice factors as parental involvement and ability are taken into account (see adjusted probabilities in Figure 3.5). Net of these college-choice factors, the lowest-SES students were nearly 15 percent less likely to secure minimal college qualifications than their upper-SES counterparts. Parental involvement in a student's education is pivotal for his or her chances of fulfilling the college qualification task. Each unit increase in parental involvement accounted for an 18 percent increase in a high school student's likelihood of securing minimal college qualifications. Early planning for college also matters. Students who planned to attend a four-year institution by

**Figure 3.4. Average Standardized Test Scores
in Math and Reading for Eighth Graders by SES**

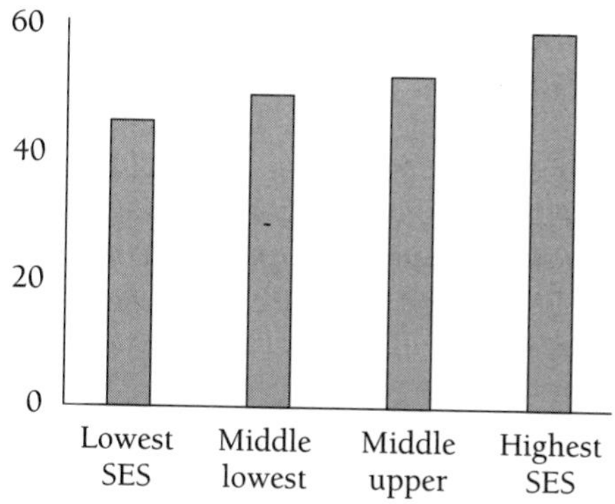

the time they were in the eighth grade were 17 percent more likely to secure minimal college qualifications by the end of the senior year. On the negative side and regardless of SES, those with at-risk factors such as coming from single-parent families, having siblings who dropped out of high school, changing schools, having poor academic performance, or repeating grades decreased the chance of becoming college qualified by 11 percent.

High School Graduation. The rate at which students complete their high school education correlates with their SES ($r = .291$). The high school graduation rate among the poorest high school students was 73 percent, a figure that sharply contrasts with the 98 percent graduation rate exhibited by the high-SES students (see actual probabilities in Figure 3.6). This 16 percent gap in the graduation rate narrows to nearly half once college-choice factors are considered (see adjusted probabilities in Figure 3.6). Securing college qualifications most influenced completing high school. Across all SES categories, securing college qualifications increased the chance of completing high school by 11.4 percent. The critical role played by college qualifications was particularly evident among the lowest-SES students. For them, chances of completing high school increased by nearly 26 percent when minimal college qualifications were obtained by the student's senior year.

Applying to College. Applying to college varies in direct relation with SES ($r = .414$). In the aggregate, differences in college application rates between the poorest and the highest-SES high school students are vast. Whereas 21.3 percent of the socioeconomically disadvantaged high school students applied to college, 76 percent of upper-SES high school students submitted college applications to four-year institutions (see actual probabilities in Figure 3.7). Controlling for relevant encouragement, qualifications, and other college-choice factors reduced the gap in college application rates between lowest-SES and upper-SES students from 55 percent to 26.4 percent (see adjusted probabilities in Figure 3.7). Although high socioeconomic

Figure 3.5. Probabilities of Securing at Least Minimal College Qualifications by the Twelfth Grade by SES (actual and adjusted)

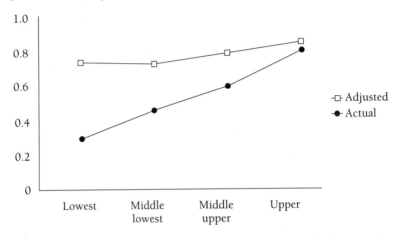

Note: Adjusted probabilities are estimated using a logistic regression model controlling for background, ability, parental involvement, college plans, and at-risk factors.

Figure 3.6. Probabilities of Securing a High School Diploma by SES (actual and adjusted)

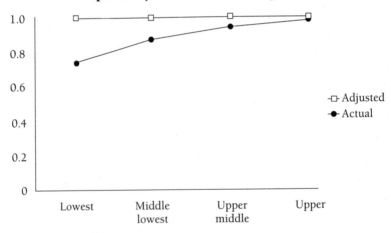

Note: Adjusted probabilities are estimated using a logistic regression model controlling for background, ability, parental involvement, college plans, and at-risk factors.

Figure 3.7. Probabilities of Applying to a Four-Year Institution by SES (actual and adjusted)

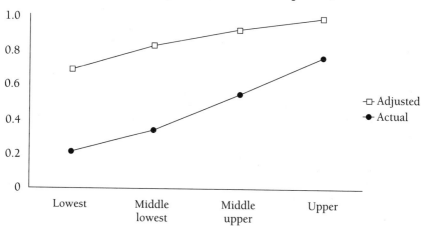

Note: Adjusted probabilities are estimated using a logistic regression model controlling for background, ability, parental involvement, college plans, and at-risk factors within each SES quartile.

backgrounds bestow high school students with a clear advantage, it is evident that motivation and college qualifications as well as family- and school-based resources all boost students' likelihood of applying to a four-year institution. High school students who aspired for at least a bachelor's degree were nearly 28 percent more likely to apply to college than those holding lower formal education aspirations. Plans to obtain an advanced degree increased application rates still further, by 34 percent. High school students whose parents held expectations for them to earn a bachelor's degree were 26 percent more prone to apply to college. Securing college qualifications during high school increased students' chances of applying to a four-year college or university by 14 percent. High school resources devoted to assisting the college application process also make a difference. Seniors who relied on high school counselors for assistance with writing college application essays and filing paper work were 8 percent and 11 percent more likely to apply to college, respectively. Information about financial aid also helps. Every unit increase in the amount of information the senior had regarding financial aid enhanced his or her chances to apply to college by 5 percent.

What Can Be Done?

Our results clearly show that intervention strategies seeking to increase college participation rates among socioeconomically disadvantaged high school students need to be holistic. Given the high degree of interdependence between family- and school-based resources, it is unrealistic to assume that one single-shot policy by itself would facilitate their success on the path to college.

Targeting the acquisition of college qualifications seems to be a most fruitful area for policy intervention. Its importance reverberates in two out of the three tasks examined by this study. The critical importance of being college qualified extends well beyond the application process. As masterfully shown by Adelman (1999a), the academic resources secured at the elementary and secondary education levels make completion of a college degree a certainty. Programs must ensure that sixth, seventh, and eighth graders and especially their parents are aware of curricula needed to succeed in college.

Becoming college qualified, in turn, presupposes high parental involvement in school activities as well as early planning for college (Henderson and Berla, 1994). And as our literature review shows (see Chapter Two), parental involvement is directly related to the amount of information that parents themselves have regarding college. Firsthand exposure to postsecondary education greatly facilitates access to this information. College-educated parents are more likely to see the long-term benefits associated with a college degree and to communicate this information to their children (Coleman, 1988). They are also more knowledgeable of the curricular requirements and mechanisms to finance college education (Flint, 1992, 1993; McDonough, 1997). In this respect, lowest-SES students are most disadvantaged. Whereas 99.3 percent of upper-SES parents have some formal college education, barely 23 percent of lowest-SES parents have been exposed to higher education (see Table 3.1). It stands to reason that information efforts targeting lowest-SES parents would yield the highest payoff.

Parental involvement in children's school activities as well as parental educational expectations are likely to be enhanced if lowest-SES parents see a connection between a college degree and economic and social benefits. Equally important is parental knowledge of curricular strategies and financial planning needed to meet the goal of securing a college education. Information on financial planning need not be detailed; providing parents with general, concise, and clear data on college costs and financial aid may suffice to motivate them to start saving for their children's postsecondary education and to learn about different financial aid packages (Hossler, Schmit, and Vesper, 1999; Olivas, 1985). A plausible source of this information is the postsecondary institution itself (Adelman, 1999). Colleges and universities are in the unique position of explaining to parents the importance of curriculum planning as early as the eighth grade. They are well aware of the specific academic skills and knowledge needed to undertake different academic majors. Moreover, colleges and universities' expertise with financial aid application procedures uniquely qualify them to assist lowest-SES parents to overcome their fears of qualifying for need-based financial aid (Olivas, 1985).

School partnerships, as early as the elementary level, constitute another promising domain in which parental involvement can be fostered the most.

A lowest-SES student's acquisition of study habits, literacy skills, and commitment to lifelong learning seems to be fostered the most when involvement comes from both parents and schools (Clark, 1983). Partnerships have an extra advantage: they provide the information and skills that lowest-SES parents themselves may need to become involved in decisions pertaining to curricular planning and school activities for their own children (Henderson and Berla, 1994)

Being aware of the curriculum and other college-related requirements one needs to meet may not suffice when the elementary and secondary institutions do not provide what Adelman (1999b, p. 47) dubs an "opportunity-to-learn." As noted by McDonough (1997), differences in college attendance rates among varied SES groups can be explained in part by the quality of the high school they attended. Little change would take place if the nation's lowest-SES students were to attend schools lacking labs, engaging and adequate curriculum, innovative instructional techniques, qualified teachers, appropriate computer equipment, books, and academic and career advising to make this opportunity-to-learn a vibrant reality.

The Talent Search Program: A Beacon of Hope

Based on the findings of our analysis, it stands to reason that programs that focus their attention on those factors enabling students to successfully complete the three critical tasks on their path to college will most benefit lowest-SES students. The Talent Search Program seems to be an example of one such program.

In 1965 the Talent Search program, originating in the Higher Education Act, was created to help low-income Americans whose parents lack college education offset institutional and sociological disadvantages on their path to college. In so doing, this program sought to identify talented individuals and help them to improve their college preparation, complete secondary school, and enroll in postsecondary education (Trent, 1992). When crafting the Talent Search program, legislators emphasized the three critical tasks investigated by this study.

In recent years, a vast body of literature has confirmed the insight and wisdom of those early policymakers (Becker, 1999). Indeed, children are more likely to succeed on their path to college when parents are involved in their learning both at home and at school (Henderson and Berla, 1994). This report also confirms the efficacy of the three-part emphasis. When we examine Talent Search participation among lowest-SES students in the NELS database, we find that two out of the three objectives are being met (see Figure 3.8).

TRIO participants were approximately 24 percent more likely to become college qualified. Though small, the correlation between Talent Search participation and securing at least minimal college qualifications is positive ($r = .229$). There are no distinctions in the high school graduation rates between participants and nonparticipants ($r = -.076$). However, Talent

Figure 3.8. Percentage Differences in Securing College Qualifications, Graduating from High School, and Applying to College Among Lowest-SES Students Based on Participation in the Talent Search Program

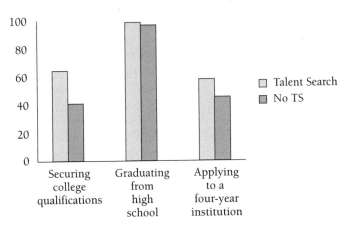

Note: Participation rates estimated via panel weight from the National Educational Longitudinal Study of 1988 (NCES, 1996) (F3PNLWT).

Search participants were almost 14 percent more likely to apply to a four-year institution immediately following high school graduation. The correlation between participation and applying to a four-year institution is small but positive ($r = .135$). Of these three relationships, the one between Talent Search participation and securing college qualifications is the strongest. In light of this evidence, intervention strategies that involve the family, the student, the community, and the school are likely to facilitate access among disadvantaged students.

Note

1. Logistic regression results are available upon request from Alberto F. Cabrera (e-mail: afc4@psu.edu).

References

Adelman, C. *Answers in the Tool Box: Academic Intensity, Attendance Patterns, and Bachelor's Degree Attainment.* Washington, D.C.: Office of Educational Research and Improvement, U.S. Department of Education, 1999a.

Adelman, C. "The Rest of the River." *University Business,* 1999b, January/February, 43–48.

Becker, J. *Partnerships with Families Promote TRIO Student Achievement.* Washington, D.C.: Opportunity Outlook, Council for Opportunity in Education, 1999.

Bernal, E. M., Cabrera, A. F., and Terenzini, P. T. "The Relationship Between Race and Socioeconomic Status (SES): Implications for Institutional Research and Admissions Policies." Paper presented before the annual meeting of the Association for Institutional Research, Cincinnati, Ohio, May 2000.

Chen, X., and Kaufman, P. "Risk and Resilience: The Effects of Dropping Out of High School." Paper presented at the annual meeting of the American Educational Research Association, Chicago, Illinois, April 1997.

Clark, R. M. *Family Life and School Achievement*. Chicago: University of Chicago Press, 1983.

Coleman, J. S. "Social Capital in the Creation of Human Capital." *American Journal of Sociology*, 1988, 94(supplement), 95–120.

Flint, T. A. "Parental and Planning Influences on the Formation of Student College Choice Sets." *Research in Higher Education*, 1992, 33(6), 689–708.

Flint, T. A. "Early Awareness of College Financial Aid: Does It Expand Choice?" *Review of Higher Education*, 1993, 16(3), 309–327.

Henderson, A. T., and Berla, N. *A New Generation of Evidence: The Family Is Critical on Student Achievement*. Washington, D.C.: National Committee for Citizens in Education, 1994.

Hossler, D., Braxton, J., and Coopersmith, G. "Understanding Student College Choice." In John C. Smart (ed.), *Higher Education: Handbook of Theory and Research*. Vol. 5. New York: Agathon Press, 1989.

Hossler, D., Schmit, J., and Vesper, N. *Going to College: How Social, Economic, and Educational Factors Influence the Decisions Students Make*. Baltimore: Johns Hopkins University Press, 1999.

King, J. E. *The Decision to Go to College: Attitudes and Experiences Associated with College Attendance Among Low-Income Students*. Washington, D.C.: The College Board, 1996.

McDonough, P. M. *Choosing Colleges: How Social Class and Schools Structure Opportunity*. Albany: State University of New York Press, 1997.

National Center for Education Statistics (NCES). National Educational Longitudinal Study of 1988. Restricted file. Washington, D.C.: National Center for Education Statistics, U.S. Department of Education, 1996. (NCES 96–130)

Olivas, M. A. "Financial Aid Packaging Policies: Access and Ideology." *Journal of Higher Education*, 1985, 56(4), 462–475.

Trent, W. T. *Measuring Program Impact: What Impacts Are Important to Assess, and What Impacts Are Possible to Measure? A Proposal for Research*. Washington, D.C.: Design Conference for the Evaluation of Talent Search, Office of Policy and Planning, U.S. Department of Education, 1992.

Alberto F. Cabrera is associate professor and senior researcher with the Center for the Study of Higher Education at Pennsylvania State University.

Steven M. La Nasa is a graduate research assistant and doctoral candidate with the Center for the Study of Higher Education at Pennsylvania State University.

4

This chapter investigates factors that facilitate postsecondary enrollment for subpopulations of high school students. Students that find themselves at risk and those with parents who have no college experience receive primary consideration.

Transition to College: What Helps At-Risk Students and Students Whose Parents Did Not Attend College

Susan P. Choy, Laura J. Horn, Anne-Marie Nuñez, Xianglei Chen

More and more high school students are being advised by their parents, teachers, and counselors to go to college. In 1990, 83 percent of high school sophomores reported that their mothers had advised them to go to college, up from 65 percent of sophomores in 1980 (Wu, 1993). During this same ten-year period, the proportion of sophomores whose teachers and counselors gave this same advice about doubled, from 32 to 65 percent. Students appear to have listened. Nearly all 1992 high school graduates (97 percent) reported that they expected to continue their education at some point, and 79 percent planned to do so immediately after finishing high school (Berkner and Chavez, 1997). By 1994, two years after they had graduated, 75 percent had enrolled in some form of postsecondary education, and 45 percent had enrolled in a four-year college.

Despite the high aspirations and enrollment rates of this cohort overall, students with certain characteristics had enrolled in four-year colleges by 1994 at substantially lower rates than others. This chapter focuses on two such groups: students whose family backgrounds and early education experiences had put them at risk of not even completing high school and students whose parents had not gone to college (that is, neither parent had any education beyond high school). It synthesizes the findings of several studies that describe behaviors and practices that appear to increase the college-going rates of these two groups (see Horn, 1997; Horn and Chen, 1998; Horn and Nuñez, 2000). Although these studies examine enrollment in all types of postsecondary education, only findings related to four-year college attendance are discussed here. Thus, all references in this chapter to students' college enrollment refer to four-year colleges only.

The data for these studies were drawn from the National Educational Longitudinal Study of 1988 (NELS), which began with a survey of a nationally representative sample of 1988 eighth graders. Follow-up surveys conducted in 1990, 1992, and 1994 captured this cohort's high school experiences and transition to college. More information on this survey (NCES, 1996a) and how to use it are provided at the end of this chapter.

Overview of the Two Groups

Based on analysis of the NELS cohort, certain characteristics have been shown empirically to put students at risk of not completing high school (Chen and Kaufman, 1997). Some of these characteristics are related to family background: being in the lowest–socioeconomic status (SES) quartile, coming from a single-parent family, and having an older sibling who dropped out of high school. Other characteristics are related to school experiences: changing schools two or more times (other than the natural progression from one level to the next), earning average grades of C or lower from sixth to eighth grades, and repeating one or more grades between first and eighth. Each of these characteristics independently increased the risk of dropping out of high school. Among the 1992 high school graduates, about one-quarter had been at moderate to high risk of not completing high school (Figure 4.1): 16 percent had been at moderate risk (two risk factors), and 9 percent had been at high risk (three or more).

The same characteristics that put students at risk of not completing high school are associated with lower college-going rates. Only 35 percent of the 1992 high school graduates with any risk factors had enrolled in college by 1994, compared with 63 percent of graduates with no risk factors (Figure 4.2). Furthermore, the more risk factors they had, the less likely they were to have enrolled. Each risk factor was independently associated with a lower likelihood of going to college, but the risk factors were interrelated and cumulative in effect (Horn, 1997). Because the number of risk factors is more important than what they are, the focus here is on the number.

Having parents who had not attended college is another characteristic that reduces the likelihood of going to college. If these students enroll in college, they are typically called *first-generation students* because they are the first generation in their immediate family to attend college. Twenty-seven percent of the 1992 high school graduates were in this category (Figure 4.1). By 1994, the college enrollment rate of the graduates whose parents had not gone to college was only 27 percent, compared with 42 percent for those whose parents had some college and 71 percent for those whose parents were college graduates (Figure 4.2). Parents' education is defined here with reference to the highest level attained by either parent. *No college* means that

Figure 4.1 Percentage Distribution of 1992 High School Graduates, According to Risk Status and Parents' Education

Risk Status

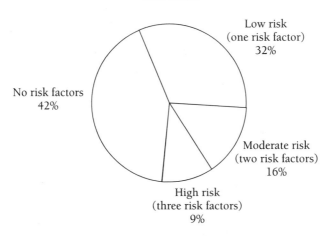

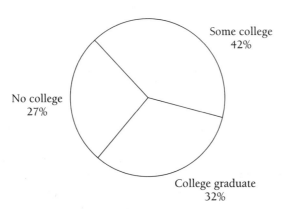

Note: Percentages may not sum to totals because of rounding.

Source: Horn and Chen, 1998, Figure 1, and Horn and Nuñez, 2000, Figure 1, based on data from National Center for Education Statistics, U.S. Department of Education, National Educational Longitudinal Study of 1988–1994, Data Analysis System (NCES, 1996b).

**Figure 4.2. Percentage of 1992 High School Graduates
Who Enrolled in a Four-Year College by 1994**

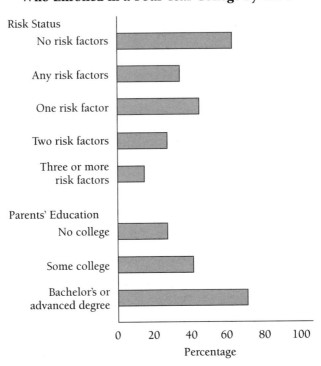

Source: Horn, 1997, Table 5, and Horn and Nuñez, 2000, Table 8 based on data from National Center for Education Statistics, U.S. Department of Education, National Educational Longitudinal Study of 1988–1994, Data Analysis System (NCES, 1996b).

neither parent had any education beyond high school; *some college* means that at least one parent had some postsecondary education but that neither had earned a bachelor's degree or higher; and *college graduate* means that at least one parent had earned a bachelor's or advanced degree.

The two groups discussed here (that is, those at risk of dropping out of high school and those whose parents did not attend college) overlap considerably. As the number of risk factors increased, so did the likelihood of having parents who had not attended college: 35 percent of students with any risk factors had parents who had not gone to college, as did 43 percent of those with two risk factors and 58 percent of those with three or more (Horn, 1997). Conversely, 80 percent of students whose parents had not gone to college had at least one risk factor: 32 percent had one, 27 percent had two, and 21 percent had three or more (NCES, 1996b). Students whose parents had no college experience averaged 2.0 risk factors, compared with 1.6 for those whose parents had some college and 1.3 for those whose parents were college graduates. In terms of their college enrollment rates, students whose parents had not gone to college most closely resembled those with two risk factors (the rate was 27 percent in both cases).

When They Leave the Pipeline to College

Practically speaking, the pipeline to college has five sequential steps. To make it through, students must (1) aspire to a bachelor's degree early enough to take the necessary preparatory steps (considered here to be during tenth grade), (2) prepare academically to a minimal level of qualification,[1] (3) take admission examinations (SAT or ACT), (4) apply to a four-year college, and (5) gain acceptance and enroll. About 40 percent of 1992 high school graduates made it through the pipeline successfully and enrolled in a four-year college (Table 4.1). Another 5 percent enrolled in a four-year college but did not have a bachelor's degree goal while in tenth grade, indicating that they changed their minds after they reported their aspirations in tenth grade (Horn, 1997). This 5 percent is not included in the analysis of progress through the pipeline.

Table 4.1 shows the percentages of students who successfully completed each step. The decline in the percentage of students as they progressed through the pipeline indicates how many students were lost at each step. The largest loss of students was at the first step, entering the pipeline by aspiring to a bachelor's degree while in tenth grade. Forty-four percent of high school graduates with any risk factors never entered the pipeline to college. Fifty-six percent of these graduates did enter, compared with 81 percent of those with no risk factors. The next largest loss occurred because students were not prepared academically: the proportion of students with any risk factors who both aspired to a bachelor's degree and were prepared academically was 44 percent (meaning that 12 percent more dropped out of the pipeline at this step), compared with 75 percent for those with no risk factors.

Additional, although smaller, losses from the pipeline occurred because some of the remaining students did not take the admission examinations, gain acceptance to a four-year institution, or enroll despite aspiring to a bachelor's degree and being academically qualified for admission (about 4 to 5 percent more dropped out at each step). By 1994, 30 percent of the graduates with any risk factors had enrolled in college, which is barely half of those who had aspired to a bachelor's degree when they were in tenth grade. In comparison, 58 percent of those with no risk factors had enrolled, which is almost three-quarters of those who had aspired to a bachelor's degree.

At each step, students were less likely to stay in the pipeline as the number of risk factors increased. The percentage of students who stayed in the pipeline to the end and did enroll declined from 39 percent of those with only one risk factor to 21 percent of those with two risk factors and to 10 percent of those with three or more risk factors.

Students whose parents had not gone to college appeared to be as successful as students who had two risk factors (moderate risk) in progressing

Table 4.1. Percentage of 1992 High School Graduates Who Progressed Through Each Step to Enrollment in a Four-Year College by 1994

	Step 1 *Tenth-Grade Bachelor's Degree Aspirations*	Step 2 *At Least Minimally Prepared Academically*	Step 3 *Took SAT or ACT*	Step 4 *Applied to Four-Year Institution*	Step 5 *Enrolled in Four-Year Institution by 1994*[a]
Total	66	56	52	47	40
Risk status					
No risk factors	81	75	73	66	58
Any risk factors	56	44	40	35	30
Low risk (one risk factor)	64	54	51	45	39
Moderate risk (two risk factors)	49	36	31	26	21
High risk (three or more risk factors)	39	23	19	16	10
Parents' education					
No college	46	33	29	25	21
Some college	64	53	49	42	35
College graduate	86	79	78	73	65

Note: To be included in the second through fifth columns, students must have been included in all previous columns.

[a]Percentages differ from Figure 4.1 because the students who did not have a bachelor's degree goal in the tenth grade(that is, did not complete Step 1) are not included (5 percent).

Source: Horn, 1997, Table 6, and National Center for Education Statistics, U.S. Department of Education, National Educational Longitudinal Study of 1988–1994 Data Analysis System (NCES, 1996b).

through each step (as indicated above, they had an average of two risk factors). They were much less likely than their peers with more educated parents to complete any of the steps. Compared with those students whose parents were college graduates, they were only about half as likely to aspire to a bachelor's degree when they were in tenth grade (46 percent versus 86 percent) and only about one-third as likely to enroll in a four-year college (21 percent versus 65 percent).

Because the greatest numbers of students leave the pipeline owing to their failure to complete the first two steps, this analysis suggests that efforts to increase college access might have the largest payoff when targeted toward encouraging students to aspire to a college degree and helping them prepare academically. However, because some students who are both motivated and prepared nevertheless leave the pipeline at later stages, assisting them with the application process, picking an appropriate college, and assembling the necessary financial resources would also help boost enrollment rates and would probably be much easier and less costly to accomplish.

What Makes a Difference

Our analyses of the NELS data suggest that parents, peers, and school personnel can all contribute to increasing the college enrollment rates of students at risk of dropping out of high school and of students whose parents had no college experience. Although reaching similar general conclusions, the analyses of the two groups have slightly different perspectives and therefore can inform us in different ways.

The analysis of at-risk students sought to explain why some students identified as being at risk of school failure manage to succeed in school and enroll in college despite their social and educational disadvantages. The analysis focused on a specific subset of 1992 high school graduates—those at moderate to high risk of not completing high school—and examined how the experiences of those who made it to college differed from those who did not. This type of comparison of at-risk graduates can provide important insights into what could be done to increase the success rate of those who did not enroll.

The analysis of students whose parents did not go to college included all the 1992 high school graduates. It compared the mathematics curricula and college preparation activities of students whose parents did not go to college with those of their counterparts whose parents had more education. Understanding the differences can help educators and policymakers identify effective ways to improve college access for students who may be at a disadvantage because their parents have no firsthand college experience. Because students' academic achievement and performance tend to vary with their parents' education, the analysis controlled for academic ability while examining the effects of parents' education.

Graduates Who Had Been at Moderate to High Risk of Dropping Out of High School

Even though graduates who had been at moderate to high risk of dropping out of high school enrolled in college at a lower rate than their peers who had not been at risk, 27 percent of 1992 high school graduates at moderate risk (two risk factors) and 14 percent at high risk (three or more risk factors) managed to enroll (Figure 4.2). To understand better the experiences of the students who were successful, compared with those who were not, we investigated how certain engagement behaviors of students, their parents, and their peers and participation in college preparation activities affect the likelihood of enrolling in a four-year college. Many of the variables had a significant positive effect on enrollment. These engagement indicators, originally found to be important for keeping students from dropping out of high school, were also important for increasing the chances of at-risk graduates who made it through high school going to college. Before introducing the results, we describe the variables used and the method of analysis.

Student Engagement with School. The level of school attendance and the number of extracurricular activities in which graduates had participated were used as indicators of their engagement in school. The attendance variable was an index based on a factor analysis of several items, including how many times they had been late for school, skipped school, or been absent. Students were characterized as having low, moderate, or high attendance, with the twenty-fifth and seventy-fifth percentiles being the cutoffs for low and high attendance, respectively. Extracurricular activities that were tallied included sports, band, theater, student government, academic societies, yearbook, service clubs, and hobby clubs.

Parent Engagement with Student Learning. Parent engagement indicators included their educational expectations for their child and how involved they were with their child's schooling. The involvement indicator was based on a factor analysis that incorporated how frequently parents discussed certain matters with their child: selecting high school courses, school activities of particular interest to their child, topics the child had studied in class, plans for taking college entrance exams, and applying to colleges. Parents were characterized as having little or no, some, or much discussion with their children (with the twenty-fifth and seventy-fifth percentiles being the cutoffs for little or no and much, respectively).

Peer Engagement with Learning. The analysis included two measures of peer engagement with learning: the degree of importance that students believed their friends attributed to learning activities and how many of the students' friends planned to attend a four-year college. The learning activities indicator was based on a factor analysis of how important they thought their friends considered certain activities: attending classes, getting good grades, finishing high school, and continuing their education past high school. The friends' engagement with learning was categorized as not very, moderately, or highly important (with the twenty-fifth and seventy-fifth percentiles being the cutoffs for not very and highly, respectively).

College Preparation Activities. Students reported whether they had participated in certain college preparation activities, including gathering information about financial aid, participating in outreach programs such as Upward Bound or Talent Search, making special efforts to prepare for college entrance examinations (including use of classes, tutoring, books, or computer programs), and receiving help from teachers or other school personnel in preparing college and financial aid applications.

Enrolling in a Four-Year College. Enrolling in a four-year college was the outcome variable used for the analysis of the effects of the engagement and preparation variables. Because the outcome measure was dichotomous (enrolling or not enrolling), a logistic regression was used.[2] Owing to their relationship to enrollment, the six risk factors and student achievement were controlled for. Two student achievement measures were included: the cumulative score from a battery of tests in mathematics, reading, science, and social science administered in eighth grade and the highest level of mathematics taken in high school. (Eight levels were constructed, ranging from a low of no mathematics to a high of completing calculus.)

Some of the engagement and participation variables may be interrelated. For example, when parents have high expectations, students may be more engaged in school. Therefore, the four sets of variables were entered into the logistic regressions hierarchically, starting with parent engagement and then adding, in turn, student engagement, peer engagement, and college preparation activities. This made it possible to see how the effect of one set of engagement variables changed as the next was introduced.

The logistic regression results are presented in terms of odds ratios (Table 4.2). For graduates who had been at moderate or high risk of not completing high school, these ratios describe the relative odds of their enrolling in a four-year college when they had a particular characteristic (such as having parents who frequently discussed school-related matters with them) compared with a reference group (such as those who had infrequent discussions with their parents). Because the odds ratios were computed after controlling for risk factors, student achievement, and the other variables in the table, they represent the independent effects of each variable shown.

Results. Peer group effects were especially strong. In fact, having friends with college plans was the strongest predictor of college enrollment. If most or all of their friends had college plans, the odds of moderate- to high-risk students enrolling in college were four times higher than if none of their friends planned to go to college.

Parental involvement was also important in predicting enrollment. The odds of enrolling in college were almost twice as great for students whose parents frequently discussed school-related matters with them as for those whose parents had little or no discussion with them. Parents' educational expectations

Table 4.2. Four-Step Logistic Regression for Probability of Moderate-to High-Risk Students Attending a Four-Year College Predicted by Parent Engagement, Student Engagement, Friends' Engagement with Learning, and College Preparation Activities (N = 2,878)

Predicted Variable[a]	Odds Ratio for At-Risk Students Attending Four-Year College Versus Other			
	Step 1	Step 2	Step 3	Step 4
Parent engagement with student's learning				
Parents discussed school-related matters with student				
Missing	0.93	0.93	0.87	0.87
Some discussion	1.51	1.41	1.36	1.31
Much discussion	2.16[b]	2.11[b]	1.97[b]	1.84[c]
Little to no discussion (comparison group)				
Parents' educational expectations for student				
Missing	1.54	1.44	1.23	1.35
Vocational or trade	0.78	0.71	0.78	0.80
Some college	1.50	1.41	1.27	1.22
Bachelor's degree	2.30	2.12	1.82	1.70
Advanced degree	1.93	1.77	1.46	1.30
High school diploma or less (comparison group)				
Student engagement with school				
Student's class attendance				
Missing		1.03	0.85	0.82
Moderate attendance		1.28	1.16	1.05
High attendance		1.49	1.38	1.25
Low attendance (comparison group)				
Extracurricular activities student participated in				
Missing		1.68	1.52	1.26
One		1.22	1.04	1.07
Two		1.86[b]	1.51	1.40
None (comparison group)				
Friends' engagement with learning				
Importance of learning to student's friends				
Missing			1.92	1.64
Moderately important			1.19	1.15
Highly important			1.19	1.15
Not very important (comparison group)				
Number of friends who planned to attend a four-year college				
Missing			2.78	3.31[b]
Few to some			1.79	1.50
Most to all			4.91[b]	4.00[b]
None (comparison group)				

Table 4.2 (*continued*)

Predicted Variable[a]	Odds Ratio for At-Risk Students Attending Four-Year College Versus Other			
	Step 1	Step 2	Step 3	Step 4
College preparation activities				
Amount of aid information used by student				
Missing				0.71
One				1.01
Two or more				1.27
None (comparison group)				
Number of people student talked to about aid				
Missing				0.78
One				1.45
Two				1.41
Three				1.36
Four or more				1.18
None (comparison group)				
Participated in any high school outreach program				
Yes				1.97[c]
No (comparison group)				
Student got help preparing for entrance exam				
Missing				0.68
Yes				1.82[b]
No (comparison group)				
Student received help from school with college application process				
Missing				2.66
Yes				1.39[c]
No (comparison group)				

Note: Results in this table were estimated by the SUDAAN software, using the weight F3QWT92G. The χ^2 values for each respective step are 710.95, 735.55, 823.03, and 896.56. All are significant at $p \leq .01$.

[a]Each logistic regression controlled for six risk factors—SES, number of times of changing school, grade point average from grades 6 to 8, single-parent family, ever held back, having one or more siblings who dropped out of school, and two achievement measures including the eighth-grade combined math, reading, science, and social studies test scores and level of mathematics courses taken over the four years of high school.

[b]$p \leq .01$.

[c]$p \leq .05$.

Source: Horn and Chen, 1998, Table 7, based on data from National Center for Education Statistics, U.S. Department of Education, National Educational Longitudinal Study of 1988–1994 Data Analysis System (NCES, 1996b).

did not appear to affect the odds of enrolling. One possible explanation may be that parents' expectations for their children are generally high, especially when their children are academically prepared for college (Horn, 1997). Consequently, expectations may vary little after controlling for students' achievement level.

College preparation activities were also related to enrollment. The odds of students who participated in any high school outreach program enrolling were about twice the odds of students who did not participate. Getting help from teachers or other school staff in applying for college also made a difference. Students who reported getting help in filling out their college applications or preparing for entrance examinations had higher odds of enrolling in college than students who reported receiving no assistance.

Student participation in two or more extracurricular activities first appeared to increase the odds of enrolling in college, but when the peer engagement variables were added, the effect disappeared. The fact that colleges typically expect or encourage high school participation in extracurricular activities suggests that participation may be correlated with having friends with college plans. Student attendance was not a factor, perhaps because it is likely to be highly correlated with student achievement and parents' involvement, which were already controlled for.

Graduates Whose Parents Had No College Experience

Participating in a rigorous mathematics curriculum significantly increases the likelihood of attending college, and parents' education is strongly connected to participating in such a curriculum. High school graduates whose parents had no college experience were less likely than their peers whose parents had graduated from college to participate in a mathematics curriculum leading to college enrollment. They were also less likely to have access to and be encouraged to follow such a curriculum and less likely to work with their parents in planning for college. This was true even for students who were the best prepared academically, where one would expect parents' education to make the least difference.

Mathematics Curriculum and College Enrollment. Taking algebra in eighth grade was strongly associated with taking advanced mathematics in high school, which, in turn, was strongly associated with a higher likelihood of attending college. Taking advanced mathematics means taking at least one course beyond Algebra 2, such as Algebra 3, Trigonometry, Precalculus, Calculus, Probability, or Statistics. Overall, 22 percent of the 1992 high school graduates took algebra in eighth grade, and 39 percent took advanced mathematics in high school; however, 78 percent of those who took algebra in eighth grade later took advanced mathematics in high school (Horn and Nuñez, 2000). Among those who took advanced mathematics in high school, about three-quarters (76 percent) enrolled in college by 1994 (Table 4.3). The enrollment rate dropped to 44 percent for those who took middle-level mathematics (Algebra 2), to 16 percent for those who took

Table 4.3. Percentage of 1992 High School Graduates Who Enrolled in a Four-Year College by 1994, by Parents' Education and Mathematics Level That Student Completed

		Parents' Education		
	Total	No College	Some College	College Graduate
Total	46	27	42	71
Mathematics course level completed				
No mathematics, low or nonacademic	6	4	7	13
Middle academic I (Algebra 1 and Geometry)	16	11	15	29
Middle academic II (Algebra 2)	44	34	41	63
Advanced academic (Beyond Algebra 2)[a]	76	64	70	85

[a]Completed at least one class beyond Algebra 2 labeled "advanced" including Precalculus, Calculus, Trigonometry, Probability, Statistics, Algebra 3, and so on.

Source: Horn and Nuñez, 2000, Table 8, based on data from National Center for Education Statistics, U.S. Department of Education, National Educational Longitudinal Study of 1988–1994 Data Analysis System (NCES, 1996b).

only algebra and geometry, and to 6 percent for those whose completion level was lower than algebra and geometry. These findings indicate that taking advanced mathematics courses in high school is an important intermediate step to college enrollment and that taking algebra in eighth grade is a critical first step.

Despite the strong association between mathematics course-taking and college attendance, parents' education still mattered. Considering only students who were at the highest level of mathematics proficiency in eighth grade according to tests administered as part of NELS, students whose parents had not attended college were less likely than their peers whose parents had graduated to take algebra in eighth grade and were less likely to take any advanced mathematics in high school even if they took algebra in eighth grade (Figure 4.3). Furthermore, they were less likely to enroll in college even if they took advanced mathematics. Among students who took advanced mathematics in high school, 85 percent of those whose parents were college graduates went to college by 1994, but only 64 percent of those whose parents had no college experience did so (Table 4.3).

Although the advantage of taking algebra in eighth grade is clear, not all schools offer it as an option, and students whose parents did not go to college were especially likely to attend such schools. Among the students with the highest level of mathematics proficiency in eighth grade, 20 percent of the students whose parents had not attended college reported that algebra was not offered in their school, compared with 10 percent of those whose parents were college graduates (Horn and Nuñez, 2000).

Figure 4.3. Percentage of 1992 High School Graduates with the Highest Level of Mathematics Proficiency in Eighth Grade Who Took Alegebra in Eighth Grade and Advanced Mathematics in High School

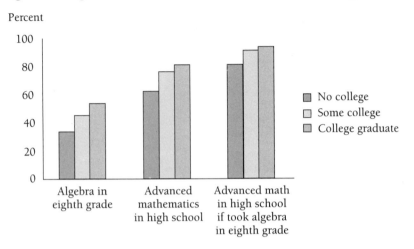

Source: Horn and Nuñez, 2000, Tables 4–6, based on data from National Center for Education Statistics, U.S. Department of Education, National Educational Longitudinal Study of 1988–1994, Data Analysis System (NCES, 1996b).

On the positive side, among students whose parents had no college experience, their mathematics curriculum significantly affected their likelihood of going to college. The more rigorous the curriculum, the more likely they were to enroll in college. For example, 64 percent of those who took advanced mathematics went to college, almost double the rate of those who stopped at Algebra 2 (34 percent) (Table 4.3). Multivariate analysis indicated that regardless of parents' education, income, academic achievement, and other related factors, students who took algebra in eighth grade improved their chances of completing advanced mathematics courses in high school. In addition, students who took such courses in high school, regardless of their level of qualification for four-year college and parents' education, income, and other factors, significantly increased their chances of enrolling in a four-year college (Horn and Nuñez, 2000). This suggests that one important way to increase the college enrollment rate of students whose parents have no college experience would be to encourage them to begin a rigorous mathematics sequence, starting with algebra in eighth grade.

Curricular Choices. To help understand why students whose parents have less education are less likely to enroll in higher-level mathematics and, later, in college, we examined how different school and family agents were involved in guiding students in selecting courses. Considering only those with the highest level of mathematics proficiency in eighth grade (thus controlling for students' ability), students whose parents did not go to college were less likely than those whose parents were college graduates to have their parents encourage them to take algebra (52 percent versus 70 percent) and more likely to choose their high school program alone (31 percent versus 22 percent) (Table 4.4).

Similarly, if students took mathematics in their senior year and took Algebra 2 or higher, their parents were less likely to be involved in their choosing a mathematics course if they had not gone to college than if they had graduated (56 percent versus 74 percent). One might expect teachers and counselors to play a more important role if the parents were not involved, but that did not seem to be the case. Similar percentages of students were advised by teachers and counselors regardless of parents' education (ranging from 55 to 62 percent).

Planning For and Applying to College. Along with being less likely to participate in a rigorous mathematics curriculum, students whose parents did not attend college were also less likely than their peers with more educated parents to participate in planning activities that lead to college enrollment, even when the students were college qualified, as defined earlier. For example, Table 4.5 shows that college-qualified students whose parents had no college experience were less likely than those whose parents had graduated from college to report that they often discussed SAT or ACT preparation (7 versus 15 percent in tenth grade and 16 versus 27 percent in twelfth grade) or postsecondary plans with their parents (41 versus 49 percent in tenth grade and 42 versus 61 percent in twelfth grade). In addition, the likelihood of college-qualified students' parents participating in the following activities increased with the parents' education: attending a program on educational opportunities for their children, attending a program about student financial aid, accompanying their child on a school visit to decide about application or enrollment, or seeking financial aid information.

Although one might expect schools to substitute for parents in some of these planning activities, this was generally not the case. There was no significant relationship between parents' education and whether college-qualified students received help from their school with various tasks associated with applying for college. Overall, 52 percent received help filling out college applications, 33 percent received help preparing an admission essay, and 46 percent received help arranging days off to visit colleges (Horn and Nuñez, 2000). College-qualified students whose parents had not attended college or had only some college were more likely than those whose parents were college graduates to report that they had received help with a financial aid application for college (51 and 47 percent versus 34 percent), but they were probably also more likely to be applying for aid.

Implications of the Findings

Students with risk factors associated with dropping out of high school and students whose parents did not attend college are less likely than other classmates to enter the college pipeline and more likely to leave the pipeline at each step along the way. Therefore, efforts to help students develop

Table 4.4. Percentage of Academically Well-Prepared 1992 High School Graduates with Access to Various Sources of Help

	Algebra in Eighth Grade[a]	High School Program[a]		Senior-Year Mathematics Course[b]		
	Parents Encouraged Student to Take	Chose with Parents	Chose Alone	Parents Helped Choose	Counselor Helped Choose	Teacher Helped Choose
Total	64	49	25	67	56	61
Parents' education						
No college	52	41	31	56	61	57
Some college	59	48	28	66	55	60
College graduate	70	52	22	74	55	62

[a]Includes only students with the highest level of mathematics proficiency in eighth grade.

[b]Includes only students who took Algebra 2 or higher in their senior year.

Source: Horn and Nuñez, 2000, Tables 10, 12, 13, based on data from National Center for Education Statistics, U.S. Department of Education, National Educational Longitudinal Study of 1988–1994 Data Analysis System (NCES, 1996b).

college aspirations early, encourage them to follow a rigorous academic curriculum, and support them through the application and enrollment process all have the potential to keep students in the pipeline and improve college enrollment rates. The largest payoffs will come from helping students to enter the pipeline and persist through the second step (preparing academically) because of the large numbers who leave then.

For moderate- to high-risk students, parental involvement was convincingly linked to an increased likelihood of attending college. The odds of enrolling in college were almost twice as great for students whose parents frequently discussed school-related matters with them compared with those of students whose parents rarely did so. Peer influence was a strong factor for these students as well. If most or all of their friends planned to go to college, they were much more likely to enroll themselves.

The analysis of the relationship between mathematics course-taking and college enrollment demonstrated the increased enrollment rates associated with following a rigorous mathematics curriculum, regardless of any other background characteristics, including parents' education. Preferably, such a curriculum would begin with algebra in eighth grade but definitely would include advanced mathematics courses in high school.

The findings of the analyses reported here suggest many actions that schools can take to help students in the two groups studied to increase their likelihood of attending college. For example, schools can provide algebra in eighth grade and high-level advanced mathematics in high school and encourage students (especially those with high ability) to take those courses. They can institute outreach programs, targeting promising students

Table 4.5. Percentage of College-Qualified 1992 High School Graduates Who Planned for College with Their Parents

| | Students and Parents Discussed Often | | | | Parents Attended Programs on | | | |
| | SAT or ACT Preparation | | Postsecondary Plans | | | | Parents Visited College | Parents Sought Financial Aid Information |
	Tenth Grade	Twelfth Grade	Tenth Grade	Twelfth Grade	Educational Opportunities	Student Financial Aid		
Total	10	22	45	51	42	46	74	81
Parents' education								
No college	7	16	41	42	29	39	61	72
Some college	9	20	41	47	39	46	71	83
College graduate	15	27	49	61	51	48	82	83

Source: Horn and Nuñez, 2000, Tables 14–17, based on data from National Center for Education Statistics, U.S. Department of Education, National Educational Longitudinal Study of 1988–1994 Data Analysis System (NCES, 1996b).

whose friends may not be college bound or whose parents did not attend college or are less involved in their children's education. Schools can also help students prepare for SAT and ACT tests and help them complete their applications for admission and financial aid, focusing on students who may not get such help from their parents. This is particularly important when students' parents did not attend college and therefore may be unfamiliar with the requirements.

For students whose parents did not go to college, teachers and counselors can assist them in two ways. First, they can act as proxies for parents by helping students choose an appropriate curriculum and guiding them through the college application process, and second, they can help encourage parents to participate in their children's schooling and learn the important steps necessary so they can help their children with college-related matters.

Notes

1. The determination of academic qualification was based on the index developed by Berkner and Chavez (1997). This index is a composite measure based on high school rank in class, ACT and SAT scores, high school grades, and the 1992 NELS mathematics and reading test composites. Students were considered minimally prepared for a four-year college as long as they met at least one of the following criteria: ranked at the fifty-fourth percentile or higher in their graduating class; earned a grade point average of 2.7 or higher in academic courses; achieved a combined SAT score of at least 820 or an ACT score of at least 19; or scored at the fifty-sixth percentile or higher on the NELS test.

2. SUDAAN was used to perform the analyses. For a detailed description of this software, see Shah, Barnwell, Hunt, and LaVange (1995).

References

Berkner, L., and Chavez, L. *Access to Postsecondary Education for the 1992 High School Graduates.* Washington, D.C.: National Center for Education Statistics, U.S. Department of Education, U.S. Government Printing Office, 1997. (NCES 98–105)

Chen, X., and Kaufman, P. "Risk and Resilience: The Effects of Dropping Out of High School." Paper presented at the annual meeting of the American Educational Research Association, Chicago, Illinois, April 1997.

Horn, L. *Confronting the Odds: Students At Risk and the Pipeline to Higher Education.* Washington, D.C.: National Center for Education Statistics, U.S. Department of Education, U.S. Government Printing Office, 1997. (NCES 98–094)

Horn, L., and Chen, X. *Toward Resiliency: At-Risk Students Who Make It to College.* Washington, D.C.: Office of Educational Research and Improvement, U.S. Department of Education, 1998.

Horn, L., and Nuñez, A. *Mapping the Road to College: First-Generation Students' Math Track, Planning Strategies, and Context of Support.* Washington, D.C.: , National Center for Education Statistics, U.S. Department of Education, U.S. Government Printing Office, 2000. (NCES 2000–153)

National Center for Education Statistics (NCES). National Educational Longitudinal Study of 1988. Restricted file. Washington, D.C.: National Center for Education Statistics, U.S. Department of Education, 1996a. (NCES 96–130)

National Center for Education Statistics (NCES). *National Educational Longitudinal Study of 1988, Data Analysis System*. Washington D.C.: Office of Educational Research and Improvement, U.S. Department of Education, 1996b. (NCES 96–127)

Shah, B., Barnwell, B., Hunt, P., and LaVange, L. *SUDAAN Users Manual*. Raleigh, N.C.: Research Triangle Institute, 1995.

Wu, S. *America's High School Sophomores: A Ten Year Comparison, 1980–1990*. Washington, D.C.: National Center for Education Statistics, U.S. Department of Education, U.S. Government Printing Office, 1993. (NCES 93–087)

SUSAN P. CHOY, LAURA J. HORN, ANNE-MARIE NUÑEZ, and XIANGLEI CHEN are researchers with MPR Associates, Inc.

5

*This chapter reviews and synthesizes what is known from
prior research about racial and ethnic group differences in
college enrollment and identifies areas for intervention.
This chapter is relevant to campus administrators,
institutional researchers, and others who are interested in
raising the share of African Americans and Hispanics
who are enrolling in U.S. colleges and universities.*

Racial and Ethnic Group Differences in College Enrollment Decisions

Laura W. Perna

More African Americans and Hispanics are attending college and receiving degrees than ever before (Nettles, Perna, and Freeman, 1999). Over the past decade, the number of African American and Hispanic undergraduates enrolled in four-year colleges and universities nationwide increased by 42 percent and 161 percent, respectively, while the number of white undergraduates increased by just 1 percent (see Table 5.1). Over the same period, the number of bachelor's degrees awarded increased by 68 percent for African Americans and 186 percent for Hispanics, compared with a 7 percent increase for whites (see Table 5.2). Despite this progress, however, analyses of the Integrated Post-secondary Education Data System show that in 1997, African Americans and Hispanics were underrepresented among both undergraduates (at 11.2 percent and 10.1 percent, respectively) and bachelor's degree recipients (7.8 percent and 6.3 percent) relative to their representation in the traditional college-age population (14.3 percent and 13.7 percent) (see Tables 5.3 and 5.4).

The continued underrepresentation of African Americans and Hispanics among undergraduates and bachelor's degree recipients does not appear to be attributable to a lack of interest in or predisposition toward college. Between 1980 and 1990 the percentage of high school sophomores who reported that they expected to earn at least a bachelor's degree increased from 35 percent to 70 percent among African Americans and from 28 percent to 62 percent among Hispanics. Comparable percentages of African American and white 1990 high school sophomores expected to at least finish college (Nettles and Perna, 1997).

A review of college enrollment rates suggests that merely aspiring to complete a bachelor's degree is not sufficient to ensure actual college enrollment

NEW DIRECTIONS FOR INSTITUTIONAL RESEARCH, no. 107, Fall 2000 © Jossey-Bass Publishers

Table 5.1. Change in the Number of Undergraduates Attending Colleges and Universities Nationwide, by Race and Ethnicity: 1976, 1986, 1997

Race and Ethnicity	1976	1986	1997	Change (percentage)		
				1976–97	1976–86	1986–97
Four-year institutions						
Total	5,686,808	6,208,613	6,992,183	23	9	13
White	4,776,499	4,979,454	5,016,915	5	4	1
African American	528,036	525,134	745,872	41	–1	42
Hispanic	145,985	220,459	575,769	294	51	161
Asian	91,088	201,808	405,908	346	122	101
Public two-year institutions						
Total	3,662,648	4,338,445	5,785,472	58	18	33
White	2,898,056	3,234,766	3,878,245	34	12	20
African American	404,404	423,102	686,676	70	5	62
Hispanic	205,713	214,976	714,141	247	5	232
Asian	77,724	174,241	350,704	351	124	101

Source: Nettles, Perna, and Freeman, 1999; and analyses of Integrated Postsecondary Education Data System, Fall Enrollment Survey.

Table 5.2. Change in the Number of Bachelor's Degrees Awarded, by Race and Ethnicity: 1977, 1987, 1997

Race and Ethnicity	1977	1987	1997	Change (percentage)		
				1977–97	1977–87	1987–97
Total	919,526	991,264	1,188,385	29	8	20
White	807,665	819,435	878,929	9	1	7
African American	58,636	54,996	92,170	57	–6	68
Hispanic	18,743	26,255	75,012	300	40	186
Asian	13,793	31,771	67,452	389	130	112

Source: Nettles, Perna, and Freeman, 1999; and analyses of Integrated Postsecondary Education Data System, Fall Enrollment Survey.

Table 5.3. Distribution of Undergraduates Attending Two-Year and Four-Year Institutions Nationwide, by Race and Ethnicity: Fall 1997

Race and Ethnicity	Sex	Total		Four-Year		Two-Year	
		Number	*Percentage*	*Number*	*Percentage*	*Number*	*Percentage*
Total	Total	12,777,655	100.0	6,992,183	100.0	5,785,472	100.0
	Women	7,169,795	56.1	3,855,877	55.1	3,313,918	57.3
	Men	5,607,860	43.9	3,136,306	44.9	2,471,554	42.7
White	Total	8,895,160	69.6	5,016,915	71.8	3,878,245	67.0
	Women	4,944,752	38.7	2,734,969	39.1	2,209,783	38.2
	Men	3,950,408	30.9	2,281,946	32.6	1,668,462	28.8
African American	Total	1,432,548	11.2	745,872	10.7	686,676	11.9
	Women	891,134	7.0	463,034	6.6	428,100	7.4
	Men	541,414	4.2	282,838	4.0	258,576	4.5
Hispanic	Total	1,289,910	10.1	575,769	8.2	714,141	12.3
	Women	736,810	5.8	330,363	4.7	406,447	7.0
	Men	553,100	4.3	245,406	3.5	307,694	5.3
Asian	Total	756,612	5.9	405,908	5.8	350,704	6.1
	Women	391,244	3.1	209,015	3.0	182,229	3.1
	Men	365,368	2.9	196,893	2.8	168,475	2.9

Source: Analyses of Integrated Postsecondary Education Data System, Fall Enrollment Survey.

Table 5.4. Distribution of Degree Recipients, by Race and Ethnicity: 1997

Race and Ethnicity	Sex	Associate		Bachelor's		Master's		Doctorate		Professional	
		Number	Percentage	Number	Percentage	Number	Percentage	Number	Percentage	Number	Percentage
Total	Total	577,398	100.0	1,188,385	100.0	421,523	100.0	46,052	100.0	78,127	100.0
	Women	351,309	60.8	662,338	55.7	239,805	56.9	18,826	40.9	32,796	42.0
	Men	226,089	39.2	526,047	44.3	181,718	43.1	27,226	59.1	45,331	58.0
White	Total	421,326	73.0	878,929	74.0	288,690	68.5	27,232	59.1	58,761	75.2
	Women	165,398	28.6	393,017	33.1	118,088	28.0	14,710	31.9	35,089	44.9
	Men	255,928	44.3	485,912	40.9	170,602	40.5	12,522	27.2	23,672	30.3
African American	Total	55,261	9.6	92,170	7.8	26,957	6.4	1,794	3.9	4,308	5.5
	Women	36,285	6.3	59,404	5.0	18,509	4.4	1,029	2.2	2,519	3.2
	Men	18,976	3.3	32,766	2.8	8,448	2.0	765	1.7	1,789	2.3
Hispanic	Total	46,531	8.1	75,012	6.3	16,368	3.9	1,170	2.5	4,123	5.3
	Women	18,687	3.2	30,578	2.6	6,471	1.5	595	1.3	2,219	2.8
	Men	27,844	4.8	44,434	3.7	9,897	2.3	575	1.2	1,904	2.4
Asian	Total	25,058	4.3	67,452	5.7	17,965	4.3	2,530	5.5	7,174	9.2
	Women	10,894	1.9	31,776	2.7	8,615	2.0	1,556	3.4	3,863	4.9
	Men	14,164	2.5	35,676	3.0	9,350	2.2	974	2.1	3,311	4.2

Source: Analyses of Integrated Postsecondary Education Data System, Completions Survey.

(Perna, 2000b). The percentage of students who actually enroll in college continues to vary by racial and ethnic group, even when only those who report aspiring to earn at least a bachelor's degree are considered. Descriptive analyses of the National Educational Longitudinal Study of 1990–1994 (NCES, 1996) reveal that only about 38 percent of African American and Hispanic 1990 high school sophomores who aspired to complete at least a bachelor's degree were enrolled in a four-year institution during the fall after graduating from high school, compared with about 55 percent of whites and Asians (Perna, 2000b).

Policymakers, college and university administrators, and institutional researchers should be concerned about the lower college enrollment rates of African Americans and Hispanics relative to those of whites and Asians for several reasons. First, because smaller proportions of African Americans and Hispanics are enrolling in college, they are less likely than whites and Asians to realize the range of benefits associated with attending college and earning at least a bachelor's degree. The economic benefits include higher lifetime earnings, whereas the noneconomic benefits include a more fulfilling work environment, better health, longer life, more informed purchases, and greater participation in cultural events (Bowen, 1980, 1997; Leslie and Brinkman, 1988; McPherson, 1993). Society also loses from the lower college enrollment rates of African Americans and Hispanics because higher levels of education are associated with such public benefits as greater productivity, greater civic involvement, greater volunteerism, higher voting rates, reduced dependence on public welfare, and lower crime rates (Bowen, 1997). Moreover, the continued underrepresentation of African Americans and Hispanics among undergraduates contributes to the low representation of African Americans and Hispanics at the next stages of the educational pipeline. Table 5.4 shows that the representation of African Americans and Hispanics declines as the degree level increases. For example, African Americans received 9.6 percent of the associate degrees awarded in 1997 but only 7.8 percent of the bachelor's degrees, 6.4 percent of the master's degrees, 5.5 percent of the first-professional degrees, and 3.9 percent of the doctoral degrees. Hispanics received 8.1 percent of the associate degrees but only 6.3 percent of the bachelor's degrees, 5.3 percent of the first-professional degrees, 3.9 percent of the master's degrees, and 2.5 percent of the doctoral degrees. Addressing the lower undergraduate enrollment rates of African Americans and Hispanics is likely an important step toward increasing the representation of African Americans and Hispanics among professional and doctoral degree recipients.

What We Know About Racial and Ethnic Group Differences in College Enrollment

According to Hossler and Gallagher (1987), the process of deciding to enroll in college may be characterized as having three phases: predisposition, search, and choice. In the first phase, students decide to attend college rather than pursue other postsecondary education alternatives (for example, work, the military). In the second phase, students search for information about college, learn about particular colleges and universities, and form a choice set. In the third phase, students select an institution from the choice set in which to enroll.

Some researchers have concluded that a student's educational expectations are among the best predictors of college enrollment (Hossler, Schmit, and Vesper, 1999; McDonough, 1997). Hossler and Stage (1992) have concluded that minority status is positively related to the postsecondary plans of Indiana ninth graders only indirectly, through involvement in school activities and parental expectations after controlling for such differences as socioeconomic status and academic ability. Nonetheless, little is known about racial and ethnic group differences in the formation of educational plans. Some researchers (for example, Hurtado, Inkelas, Briggs, and Rhee, 1997) have concluded that a more precise model of the predisposition stage is required to fully understand racial and ethnic group differences in college enrollment behavior.

Relatively little is also known about racial and ethnic group differences in the search phase. Based on their analyses of data from the National Longitudinal Study of the High School Class of 1972 and the High School and Beyond Survey of 1980 and 1982 high school seniors, St. John and Noell (1989) have found that in all three classes, African Americans were more likely than whites and Hispanics to apply to college after controlling for differences in background characteristics. Using the number of applications submitted to postsecondary educational institutions as a measure of search, Hurtado, Inkelas, Briggs, and Rhee (1997) have concluded that African American and Hispanic college applicants apply to a greater number of colleges than whites after controlling for background characteristics, ability, and college preferences. The small percent of variance explained by the Hurtado, Inkelas, Briggs, and Rhee model (11 percent) suggests, however, that further examination of the search phase may improve our understanding of racial and ethnic group differences in the college enrollment process.

Although more attention has been focused on the choice phase of the process, the results of such research are inconsistent. Using data from High School and Beyond, St. John and Noell (1989) have found that college enrollment rates were comparable for African American, Hispanic, and white high school seniors after controlling for differences in background, ability, and educational aspirations. African American college applicants were less likely than their white peers to enroll, however, after also controlling for financial aid offers. Other researchers have shown that, compared with their white counterparts and after controlling for other differences, African American high school students are less likely to enroll in college (Nolfi and others, 1978), are less likely to attend highly selective colleges and universities (Hearn, 1984) and are less likely to attend their first-choice institution (Hurtado, Inkelas, Briggs, and Rhee, 1997). Still other research suggests that African Americans are more likely than whites to enroll in college (Thomas, 1980; Catsiapis, 1987; Kane and Spizman, 1994; Perna, 2000a) and tend to enroll in four-year rather than two-year colleges (Rouse, 1994; Perna, 2000b) holding constant other variables.

Researchers have also shown that the variables that predict college enrollment vary by race and ethnicity, suggesting that the college enrollment decision-making process is different for African Americans, Hispanics, and whites. For example, Hurtado and her colleagues (1997) have found that ability is a less important predictor of the number of applications to college for African Americans than for whites, Hispanics, and Asians. Thomas (1980) has found that socioeconomic status and test scores had stronger direct effects on college enrollment for African American 1972 high school seniors, particularly African American males, than for their white counterparts. St. John (1991) has concluded that African American high school seniors were more likely than white seniors to attend college when region, family background, ability, and high school experiences were controlled but were no more likely than white seniors to attend when educational expectations were also controlled. Hispanic seniors were less likely than other seniors to attend college when region and family background were controlled but as likely to do so as white seniors when test scores and high school experiences were also taken into account. Jackson (1990) has shown that receiving financial aid had a stronger positive effect on the probability of enrolling in college for African American and Hispanic college applicants in 1980 than for their white counterparts but that the positive effect of financial aid for Hispanics disappeared when background and academic characteristics were also held constant. Other research suggests that educational expectations are a less important predictor of college enrollment for African Americans than for whites (Thomas, 1980; Perna, 2000a).

Theoretical Framework for Understanding Racial and Ethnic Group Differences in College Enrollment

Among the conceptual frameworks that have been used to examine college enrollment behavior are sociological status attainment approaches (for example, Thomas, 1980; Hearn, 1984) and social-psychological approaches (for example, Chapman, 1981; Hossler, Braxton, and Coopersmith, 1989). Another common theoretical approach to examining college enrollment decisions is economic (Fuller, Manski, and Wise, 1982; Manski and Wise, 1983; Schwartz, 1985; Hossler, Braxton, and Coopersmith, 1989; Hossler, Schmit, and Vesper, 1999). Econometric models posit that an individual makes a decision about attending college by comparing the benefits with the costs for all possible alternatives and then selecting the alternative with the greatest net benefit, given the individual's personal tastes and preferences (Hossler, Braxton and Coopersmith, 1989; Manski and Wise, 1983). The short-term consumption benefits of attending college include enjoyment of the learning experience, involvement in extracurricular activities, participation in social and cultural events, and enhancement of social status. Future benefits include higher lifetime earnings, more fulfilling work environment, better health, longer life, more informed purchases, and lower probability of unemployment (Bowen, 1980, 1997; Leslie and Brinkman, 1988; McPherson, 1993). The costs of investing in a college education include the direct costs of attendance (for example, tuition, fees, room, board, books, and supplies) less financial aid, the opportunity costs of forgone earnings and leisure time, and the costs of traveling between home and the institution.

Because the informational and computational requirements implied by econometric models exceed an individual's information-processing capacities, rational models of decision making are generally regarded as normative rather than descriptive models (Hogarth, 1987). To manage cognitive decision-making demands, individuals adopt such strategies as satisficing or bounded rationality. McDonough (1997, p. 9) has used Bourdieu's concept of habitus to explain that an individual's expectations, attitudes, and aspirations are not based on rational analyses but are "sensible or reasonable choices." *Habitus,* or the internalized system of thoughts, beliefs, and perceptions acquired from the immediate environment, conditions an individual's expectations, attitudes, and aspirations (Bourdieu and Passeron, 1977; McDonough, 1997; McDonough, Antonio, and Trent, 1997).

According to the traditional econometric perspective, the decision to invest in higher education is influenced by expected costs and benefits, financial resources, academic ability, current and expected labor market opportunities, personal preferences and tastes, and uncertainty (Becker, 1962). Parental educational attainment is typically the sole (if any) proxy for differences in expectations, personal preferences and tastes, and uncertainty that is included in traditional econometric models (for example, Schwartz, 1985; Rouse, 1994). Based on her examinations of racial and ethnic group differences in college enrollment, however, Perna (2000a, 2000b) concludes that the explanatory power of the traditional econometric approach to college enrollment decisions is improved when measures of social and cultural capital are used as proxies for differences in expectations, preferences, tastes, and certainty about higher education investment decisions.

Qualitative researchers have drawn upon the sociological concepts of social and cultural capital to describe the ways in which knowledge and information about college, as well as the value placed on obtaining a college education, may influence college enrollment decisions (for example, Freeman, 1997; McDonough, 1997). Like human capital and physical capital, social and cultural capital are resources that may be invested to enhance profitability (Bourdieu and Passeron, 1977) and productivity (Coleman, 1988) and facilitate upward mobility (DiMaggio and Mohr, 1985; Lamont and Lareau, 1988). *Social capital* may take the form of information-sharing channels and networks as well as social norms, values, and expected behaviors

(Coleman, 1988). *Cultural capital* is the system of factors derived from one's parents that defines an individual's class status (Bourdieu and Passeron, 1977). Members of the dominant class possess the most economically and symbolically valued kinds of cultural capital (Bourdieu and Passeron, 1977; McDonough, 1997). Individuals who lack the required cultural capital may (1) lower their educational aspirations or self-select out of particular situations (for example, not enroll in higher education) because they do not know the particular cultural norms, (2) overperform to compensate for their less-valued cultural resources, or (3) receive fewer rewards for their educational investment (Bourdieu and Passeron, 1977; Lamont and Lareau, 1988).

Appropriateness of an Expanded Econometric Model for Understanding Racial and Ethnic Group Differences in College Enrollment

Some research has shown the value of considering social and cultural capital when examining the college enrollment behavior of African Americans. Through group interviews with African American high school students about the barriers they perceive to limit their participation in higher education, Freeman (1997) has found that African American students are uncertain about their ability to pay the short-term costs of attending and about whether the long-term economic benefits of attending would exceed those costs. Interviewees also pointed to the potential influence of the physical conditions of the schools attended by African Americans, interest and assistance from teachers and counselors, belief at an early age that pursuing postsecondary education is a realistic option, and African American role models. Many of these perceptions may be interpreted as manifestations of social and cultural capital. Based on their examination of the variables related to the decision of African American college freshmen to attend a historically black rather than a predominantly white college or university, McDonough, Antonio, and Trent (1997) conclude that traditional models of college-choice decision making must be modified for the African American habitus, their race-based set of subjective views and perceptions.

Research also suggests that the amount of social and cultural capital, as well as the strategies for converting this capital into educational attainment, differ by social class and race and ethnicity (Arnold, 1993; Lareau, 1987; Orfield, 1988). Based on her qualitative study of educational attainment among African American and Mexican American valedictorians, Arnold (1993) concludes that racial, class, and gendered social structures and cultural norms restrict educational attainment for minority students. Orfield (1988) has found that the percent of African American and Hispanic high school graduates in the Los Angeles metropolitan area who attended four-year colleges and universities declined during the early 1980s, while the percent of Asian high school graduates, many of whom were first-generation college students, increased, suggesting cultural differences in the value of educational success across racial and ethnic groups. Stanton-Salazar (1997) hypothesizes that to be socialized successfully, minority youth must learn to decode the dominant culture and participate in multiple sociocultural venues. This requires overcoming sociocultural, socioeconomic, linguistic, and structural barriers.

Perna (2000a, 2000b) tests the usefulness of an econometric model that has been expanded to include measures of social and cultural capital as proxies for differences in expectations, preferences, tastes, and uncertainty about the higher education investment decisions for understanding racial and ethnic group differences in the choice phase of the college enrollment process. Using logistic regression analyses and controlling for differences in costs, benefits, financial resources, academic ability, and social and cultural capital, Perna (2000a) has found that African American high school graduates are more likely than white and Hispanic high school graduates to attend a four-year college or university in the fall after graduating from high school. Controlling for similar variables but using multinomial logistic regression analyses, Perna (2000b) has also found that African American bachelor's degree aspirants are more likely to enroll in a four-year college or university but less likely to enroll in a public two-year institution in the fall after graduating from high school than their white, Hispanic, and Asian counterparts.

Perna (2000a) has shown that the relative contribution of social and cultural capital to the model for four-year college enrollment is different for African Americans and Hispanics than for whites. For all three groups, adding proxies for social and cultural capital to the traditional econometric model (that is, one that controls only for costs, benefits, financial resources, and academic ability) improves the fit of the model. For white high school graduates, measures of academic ability contribute most to the model fit, followed by measures of social and cultural capital and then by measures of costs, benefits, and financial resources. For African American and Hispanic high school graduates, however, the relative contribution of social and cultural capital variables is comparable to the relative contribution of academic ability variables. This research suggests that including measures of social and cultural capital as proxies for differences in expectations, preferences, tastes, and uncertainty in the traditional econometric framework is especially important for understanding the college enrollment decisions of African Americans and Hispanics (Perna, 2000a).

Implications for Practice and Research

Prior research on racial and ethnic group differences in college enrollment also has several implications for college and university admissions officers, institutional researchers, and others interested in raising the college enrollment rates of African Americans and Hispanics. For college and university admissions officers, prior research points to several types of interventions that may effectively increase college enrollment rates for underrepresented groups. One area for intervention pertains to the quality and intensity of the academic preparation of African American and Hispanic high school students (Berkner and Chavez, 1997; Horn, 1997; Adelman, 1999b; Perna, 2000b). Some evidence suggests that Asian and white high school graduates are more likely than African American and Hispanic high school graduates to be at least minimally qualified to attend college, where college qualification is an index based on high school academic grades, class rank, test scores, and rigor of the curriculum (Berkner and Chavez, 1997). Other research (Perna, 2000b) shows that the likelihood of enrolling in a four-year college or university is substantially higher for students who have taken at least one advanced mathematics course. But substantially smaller proportions of African American and Hispanic than of white and Asian bachelor's degree aspirants have taken at least one advanced mathematics course (Perna, 2000b).

One reason African Americans and Hispanics may be less likely than whites and Asians to take advanced mathematics courses is that such classes are not offered in the high schools they attend. Although some have begun to address this issue of educational equity through the courts (Hebel, 1999), possible nonlegal remedies include allowing high school students to take courses at local community colleges with credit awarded to the student from both the high school and the community college, providing additional funds to train teachers and enhance high school course offerings, and offering advanced courses on-line (Adelman, 1999a; Hebel, 1999; Perna, 2000b). Improving academic opportunities, preparation, and achievement must be a central component of any attempt to increase the college enrollment rates of underrepresented groups.

A second area for intervention that may be particularly important for raising the four-year college enrollments of Hispanics pertains to the level of parental involvement in the student's education. Although the likelihood of enrolling in a four-year college or university has been shown to increase with the level of parental involvement for both African Americans and Hispanics, the average level of parental involvement has been observed to be lower for Hispanics than for African Americans and whites (Perna, 2000b). The model of parental involvement proposed by Hoover-Dempsey and Sandler (1997) suggests that efforts to increase parental involvement must recognize that the decision to become involved in the child's education is likely a function of the parents' role construction or beliefs about appropriate behavior, the parents' sense of efficacy or confidence for helping the student succeed in school, and the parents' perception of being invited by the school and the student to participate. Beliefs about the appropriate parental role in the child's education are likely influenced by their cultural capital (Lareau, 1987). For Hispanics, parental involvement may be limited by a lack of relevant resources (for example, their own educational attainment, occupational status, work schedule flexibility) or their patterns of family life (for example, kinship ties, socialization patterns, leisure activities) (Lareau, 1987).

Many early intervention programs, programs that are designed to increase awareness of and preparation for higher education among disadvantaged students, include a parental component (Perna, Fenske, and Swail, forthcoming). For example, as part of Washington's National Early Intervention Scholarship Program, parents must spend at least four hours each month in program activities. Vermont's National Early Intervention Scholarship Program includes home visits, evening presentations, informational sessions, and college and financial aid workshops. More research is required, however, to identify the most effective ways to involve parents in these programs as well as the relationship between parental participation in such programs and actual college enrollment.

For institutional researchers and others who are interested in developing a better understanding of racial and ethnic group differences in college enrollment, one set of implications pertains to the most appropriate conceptual framework for examining these differences. As concluded by Perna (2000a, 2000b), an econometric framework that has been expanded to include measures of social and cultural capital as proxies for differences in expectations, preferences, tastes, and uncertainty appears to provide important insights into racial and ethnic group differences in college enrollment behavior. Expanding the traditional econometric model to include measures of social and cultural capital builds on McDonough's conclusion (1997) that the college-choice process does not conform to the economist's rational-choice model. By incorporating measures of social and cultural capital into the traditional econometric framework, the results of such analyses are also likely to be of greater use to college and university admissions officers and other interested individuals. With their focus on the role of family background and academic ability, the results of much of the traditional econometric research on college enrollment are often fairly pessimistic because such variables as parental education and test scores have not been amenable to public policy. In contrast, by explicitly examining the influence of social and cultural capital on college enrollment decisions, research that uses an expanded econometric model is more likely to point to the types of policies and practices that will lead to higher college enrollment rates.

One of the biggest challenges for institutional and other educational researchers is to identify the most appropriate ways to operationalize social and cultural capital. Essentially, the task is to identify variables that describe the ways in which parental education, class status, and social networks influence the college enrollment process. Perna (2000a, 2000b) has attempted to operationalize the social and cultural capital constructs described in the relevant qualitative research (for example, McDonough, 1997) using the variables available in the National Educational Longitudinal Study (NELS) database. Among the proxies that Perna (2000a, 2000b) has included as measures of social and cultural capital in the form of the availability of knowledge and information about college are the following: the share of high school graduates who enroll in a four-year college or university, the share of African Americans and Hispanics in the student body, high school control, high school location, and school assistance with college admissions requirements. Perna (2000a, 2000b) has also tested several measures of social and cultural capital in the form of the value placed on obtaining a college education including parents' expectations for the child's education, parental saving for college, parental involvement in the child's education, share of peers planning to attend a four-year college, and participation in extracurricular activities.

Although the relationship between these variables and college enrollment may suggest general areas for intervention and further attention, future research should explore the appropriateness of additional or more descriptive variables. For example, Perna (2000b) has found that four-year college enrollment rates are higher for African Americans who attend high schools in which the majority of graduates attend a four-year college than for other African Americans after controlling for differences in costs, benefits, financial resources, academic ability, and social and cultural capital. But her analyses do not reveal the ways in which this supposed measure of high school quality promotes college enrollment behavior. The results of McDonough's qualitative study (1997) of twelve white high school girls suggest that schools structure postsecondary opportunity through the timing, availability, and support for college advising, organizational mission and curriculum, assumptions of students' cultural capital, and counselor role expectations and enactment. From their analyses of data from High School and Beyond, Falsey and Heyns (1984) hypothesize that high school seniors who attend private high schools are more likely to enroll in college and enroll in four-year rather than two-year institutions after controlling for student achievement and aspirations, family characteristics, and school characteristics because of organizational policies, orientation of school support, and resources for counseling and advising. Future research should further explore the ways in which these and other characteristics can be operationalized.

A second challenge for institutional researchers is to identify the variations in this expanded econometric conceptual framework that are required to more completely understand racial and ethnic group differences in two-year college enrollment. Using multinomial logistic regression analyses to predict public two-year and four-year college enrollment relative to no enrollment, Perna (2000b) concludes that her expanded econometric model of college enrollment is substantially better for predicting four-year college enrollment decisions than for predicting public two-year college enrollment decisions. Table 5.1 shows that, among whites, African Americans, and Hispanics, undergraduate enrollment increased over the past decade at a faster rate at public two-year than at four-year colleges and universities. In 1997 African Americans, Hispanics, and Asians represented a higher share of undergraduates at two-year institutions than at four-year institutions (Table 5.3). Given these differential enrollment rates and the findings from research showing that students consider different criteria (and apply different weights to these criteria) when considering whether to attend a two-year rather than a four-year institution (Heller, 1997; Perna, 2000b), future research should focus on developing a more complete model of two-year college enrollment for students of different racial and ethnic groups.

Future research should also further explore the presence of sex differences in college enrollment among students of the same racial and ethnic group. As evinced in part by a November 1999 conference entitled "Fewer Men on Campus: A Puzzle for Liberal Arts Colleges and Universities," college leaders are becoming increasingly concerned about the growing gender imbalance in their undergraduate student bodies (Gose, 1999). Although the number of male undergraduates increased by 11 percent between 1976 and 1996, the number of female undergraduates increased at a faster rate (51 percent) (National Center for Education Statistics, 1999). Because of the differential growth rates, the representation of men among undergraduates has declined from 52 percent in 1976 to 48 percent in 1980 and to 44 percent in 1997. With the exception of nonresident aliens, the number of women undergraduates exceeds the number of men undergraduates regardless of race and ethnicity. But the magnitude of the gender gap in undergraduate enrollments varies by racial and ethnic group. In fall 1997, women represented 62 percent of African American undergraduates, compared with 52 percent of Asians, 56 percent of whites, 57 percent of Hispanics, and 59 percent of American Indians or Alaskan Natives (Table 5.3).

Based on her analyses of race and sex differences in college attendance among 1972 high school seniors, Thomas (1980) has concluded that after controlling for differences in socioeconomic status, academic characteristics, significant others' influence, and educational expectations, sex differences in the college enrollment process were greater among whites than among blacks. White men were found to be more likely than white women to enroll in college even after controlling for other variables, but among blacks, sex was unrelated to college enrollment. Among bachelor's degree aspirants in the early 1990s, however, Perna (2000b) has found that both African American and white women were more likely than their African American and white male counterparts to enroll in a four-year college even after controlling for expected costs and benefits, financial resources, academic characteristics, and social and cultural capital. These findings suggest that the observed sex differences in college enrollment may not be entirely attributable to differences between women and men in the variables that are related to college enrollment and that the relationship between sex and college enrollment may vary across racial and ethnic groups. Therefore, future research should continue to recognize the diversity of student experiences by exploring reasons for differences in college enrollment between women and men of the same racial and ethnic group.

The NELS is a useful source for examining some of the suggested areas for future research. Sponsored by the U.S. Department of Education's National Center for Education Statistics (NCES), the NELS contains data for a cohort of students when they were in the eighth grade (1988), when they were high school sophomores (1990), when they were high school seniors (1992), and two years after their scheduled high school graduation (1994). The third in the U.S. Department of Education's series of longitudinal studies examining the transition from high school to education and employment, the NELS is an invaluable source of data for those who are interested in examining racial and ethnic group differences in college enrollment behavior. The usefulness of the NELS is evidenced in part by the number of recent studies utilizing this database (for example, Hurtado, Inkelas, Briggs, and Rhee, 1997; Perna, 2000a, 2000b).

The NELS clearly has several important strengths that are relevant to research on racial and ethnic group differences in college enrollment behavior. First, it is a longitudinal database that spans the key years of the college enrollment process, from the eighth grade to two years out of high school. The NELS is also characterized by high response rates, with a weighted response rate of 91 percent to the third (1994) follow-up (Haggerty and others, 1996) and reasonably large sample sizes, with 14,915 completed cases for the third follow-up (Haggerty and others, 1996). Participating students attended more than one thousand public and private schools nationwide. The NELS includes numerous variables, including measures of background and demographic characteristics, achievement (for example, test scores and coursework), attitudes (for example, goals and values), plans (for example, educational expectations), and actual behaviors (for example, college enrollment). Moreover, data were collected not only from the participating students but also from their parents, teachers, school principals, and school records.

Institutional and other researchers must recognize that, like all data sources, the NELS is not perfect. One important weakness pertains to the small numbers of Asians and American Indians in the sample. Their small numbers restrict the conclusions that may be drawn about the college enrollment process for these groups. A second weakness is that although the NELS was designed to describe critical transitions, a number of potentially important variables pertaining to the college enrollment process are not available. For instance, one potentially important but unavailable measure of social and cultural capital is the number of siblings in college, a variable that has been found to be related to college enrollment behavior by other researchers (for example, Manski and Wise, 1983; McDonough, 1997).

Nonetheless, constructing the perfect, comparably large, nationally representative longitudinal database is cost prohibitive and an inefficient use of resources for most researchers. By using the NELS and noting its limitations, institutional and other researchers may help contribute to the development of a more perfect future NCES database. The NELS also provides an invaluable starting point from which researchers may supplement additional methodologies (for example, qualitative) and additional samples.

References

Adelman, C. *Answers in the Tool Box: Academic Intensity, Attendance Patterns, and Bachelor's Degree Attainment.* Washington, D.C.: U.S. Department of Education, Office of Educational Research and Improvement, 1999a.

Adelman, C. "The Rest of the River." *University Business,* January/February, 1999b, 43–48.

Arnold, K. D. "The Fulfillment of Promise: Minority Valedictorians and Salutatorians." *Review of Higher Education,* 1993, *16*(3), 257–283.

Becker, G. S. "Investment in Human Capital: A Theoretical Analysis." *Journal of Political Economy,* 1962, *70*(supplement)(5), 9–49.

Berkner, L., and Chavez, L. *Access to Postsecondary Education for the 1992 High School Graduates.* Washington, D.C.: National Center for Education Statistics, U.S. Department of Education, U.S. Government Printing Office, 1997. (NCES 98–105)

Bourdieu, P., and Passeron, J. C. *Reproduction in Education, Society, and Culture.* Beverly Hills, Calif.: Sage, 1977.

Bowen, H. R. *The Costs of Higher Education: How Much Do Colleges and Universities Spend per Student and How Much Should They Spend?* San Francisco: Jossey-Bass, 1980

Bowen, H. R. *Investment in Learning: The Individual and Social Value of American Higher Education* Baltimore: Johns Hopkins University Press, 1997. (Originally published 1977.)

Catsiapis, G. "A Model of Educational Investment Decisions." *Review of Economics and Statistics,* 1987, *69,* 33–41.

Chapman, D. "A Model of Student College Choice." *Journal of Higher Education,* 1981, *52*(5), 490–505.

Coleman, J. S. "Social Capital in the Creation of Human Capital." *American Journal of Sociology,* 1988, *94*(supplement), 95–120.

DiMaggio, P., and Mohr, J. "Cultural Capital, Educational Attainment, and Marital Selection." *American Journal of Sociology,* 1985, *90*(6), 1231–1261.

Falsey, B., and Heyns, B. "The College Channel: Private and Public Schools Reconsidered." *Sociology of Education,* 1984, *57*(2), 111–122.

Freeman, K. "Increasing African Americans' Participation in Higher Education: African American High School Students' Perspectives." *Journal of Higher Education,* 1997, *68*(5), 523–550.

Fuller, W. C., Manski, C. F., and Wise, D. A. "New Evidence on the Economic Determinants of Postsecondary Schooling Choices." *The Journal of Human Resources,* 1982, *17*(4), 477–498.

Gose, B. "Colleges Look for Ways to Reverse Decline in Enrollment of Men." *Chronicle of Higher Education,* November 26, 1999, p. A73.

Haggerty, C., and others. *Methodology Report: National Educational Longitudinal Study 1988–1994.* Washington, D.C.: National Center for Education Statistics, 1996.

Hearn, J. C. "The Relative Roles of Academic, Ascribed, and Socioeconomic Characteristics in College Destinations." *Sociology of Education,* 1984, *57*(1), 22–30.

Hebel, S. "A.P. Courses Are New Target in Struggle over Access to College in California." *Chronicle of Higher Education,* November 26, 1999, p. A32.

Heller, D. E. "Student Price Response in Higher Education: An Update to Leslie and Brinkman." *Journal of Higher Education,* 1997, *68*(6), 624–659.

Hogarth, R. M. *Judgment and Choice: The Psychology of Decision.* (2nd ed.) Chicago: Wiley, 1987.

Hoover-Dempsey, K., and Sandler, H. "Why Do Parents Become Involved in Their Children's Education?" *Review of Educational Research,* 1997, *67*(1), 3–42.

Hossler, D., Braxton, J., and Coopersmith, G. "Understanding Student College Choice." In John C. Smart (ed.), *Higher Education: Handbook of Theory and Research.* Vol. 5. New York: Agathon Press, 1989.

Hossler, D., and Gallagher, K. S. "Studying Student College Choice: A Three-Phase Model and the Implications for Policymakers." *College and University*, 1987, 2(3), 207–221.

Hossler, D., and Stage, F. "Family and High School Experience Influences on the Post-secondary Educational Plans of Ninth-Grade Students." *American Educational Research Journal*, 1992, 29(2), 425–451.

Hossler, D., Schmit, J., and Vesper, N. *Going to College: How Social, Economic, and Educational Factors Influence the Decisions Students Make.* Baltimore: Johns Hopkins University Press, 1999.

Hurtado, S., Inkelas, K. K., Briggs, C., and Rhee, B. S. "Differences in College Access and Choice Among Racial/Ethnic Groups: Identifying Continuing Barriers." *Research in Higher Education*, 1997 38(1), 43–75.

Jackson, G. A. "Financial Aid, College Entry, and Affirmative Action." *American Journal of Education*, 1990, 98(4), 523–550.

Kane, J., and Spizman, L. M. "Race, Financial Aid Awards, and College Attendance: Parents and Geography Matter." *American Journal of Economics and Sociology*, 1994, 53(1), 73–97.

Lamont, M., and Lareau, A. "Cultural Capital: Allusions, Gaps, and Glissandos in Recent Theoretical Developments." *Sociological Theory*, 1988, 6(Fall), 153–168.

Lareau, A. "Social Class Differences in Family-School Relationships: The Importance of Cultural Capital." *Sociology of Education*, 1987, 60(April), 73–85.

Leslie, L. L., and Brinkman, P. T. *The Economic Value of Higher Education.* New York: American Council on Education, Macmillan, 1988.

Manski, C. F., and Wise, D. A. *College Choice in America.* Cambridge: Harvard University Press, 1983.

McDonough, P. M. *Choosing Colleges: How Social Class and Schools Structure Opportunity.* Albany: State University of New York Press, 1997.

McDonough, P. M., Antonio, A. L., and Trent, J. W. "Black Students, Black Colleges: An African American College-Choice Model." *Journal for a Just and Caring Education*, 1997, 3(1), 9–36.

McPherson, M. S. "How Can We Tell If Financial Aid Is Working?" In M. S. McPherson, M. O. Shapiro, and G. C. Winston (eds.), *Paying the Piper: Productivity, Incentives, and Financing in U.S. Higher Education.* Ann Arbor: University of Michigan Press, 1993.

National Center for Education Statistics. *Digest of Education Statistics.* Washington, D.C.: National Center for Education Statistics, 1999.

National Center for Education Statistics (NCES). National Educational Longitudinal Study of 1988. Restricted file. Washington, D.C.: National Center for Education Statistics, U.S. Department of Education, 1996. (NCES 96–130)

Nettles, M. T., and Perna, L. W. *The African American Education Data Book: The Transition from School to College and School to Work.* Vol. 3. Fairfax, Va.: Frederick D. Patterson Research Institute, 1997.

Nettles, M. T., Perna, L. W., and Freeman, K. E. *Two Decades of Progress: African Americans Moving Forward in Higher Education.* Fairfax, Va.: Frederick D. Patterson Research Institute, 1999.

Nolfi, G. J., and others. *Experiences of Recent High School Graduates: The Transition to Work or Postsecondary Education.* Lexington, Mass.: Lexington Books, 1978.

Orfield, G. "Exclusion of the Majority: Shrinking College Access and Public Policy in Metropolitan Los Angeles." *The Urban Review*, 1988, 20(3), 147–183.

Perna, L. W. "Differences in College Enrollment Among African Americans, Hispanics, and Whites." *Journal of Higher Education*, 2000a, 71(2), 117–141.

Perna, L. W. "Racial/Ethnic Group Differences in the Realization of Educational Plans." Paper presented at the annual meeting of the American Educational Research Association, New Orleans, Louisiana, April 2000b.

Perna, L.W., Fenske, R. H., and Swail, W. S. "An Overview of Early Intervention Programs." In *Advances in Education Research,* National Library of Education, forthcoming.

Rouse, C. E. "What to Do After High School: The Two-Year Versus Four-Year College Enrollment Decision." In R. G. Ehrenberg (ed.), *Choices and Consequences: Contemporary Policy Issues in Education.* New York: IRL Press, 1994.

St. John, E. P. "What Really Influences Minority Attendance? Sequential Analyses of the High School and Beyond Sophomore Cohort." *Research in Higher Education,* 1991, 32(2), 141–158.

St. John, E. P., and Noell, J. "The Effects of Student Financial Aid on Access to Higher Education: An Analysis of Progress with Special Consideration of Minority Enrollments." *Research in Higher Education,* 1989, 30(6), 563–581.

Schwartz, J. B. "Student Financial Aid and the College Enrollment Decision: The Effects of Public and Private Grants and Interest Subsidies." *Economics of Education Review,* 1985, 4(2), 129–144.

Stanton-Salazar, R. D. "A Social Capital Framework for Understanding the Socialization of Racial Minority Children and Youths." *Harvard Educational Review,* 1997, 67(1), 1–40.

Thomas, G. E. "Race and Sex Differences and Similarities in the Process of College Entry." *Higher Education,* 1980, 9(2), 179–202.

LAURA W. PERNA is assistant professor in the Department of Education Policy and Leadership at the University of Maryland.

6

*This chapter reviews many of the major programs
seeking to increase college access among economically
disadvantaged and at-risk students. The author evaluates
the potential of these programs while stressing four
conditions that effective programs must meet.*

Preparing America's Disadvantaged for College: Programs That Increase College Opportunity

Watson Scott Swail

To this point, most of the chapters in this volume have focused on the college-choice process and the pathways to college for disadvantaged youth in the United States. In sum, we have learned that higher education is serving more students than at any other time in history and that more students from traditionally underrepresented groups are attending, persisting, and attaining degrees than ever before. However, we have also learned that the pathway to college is strewn with the remains of our youth who did not quite fit the bill of higher education—let alone find the means to pay for it. Despite our best efforts in terms of public policy and institutional practice, students of color and lower socioeconomic status (SES) are less likely to have attained the attributes necessary to advance to the "bonus round" in education: postsecondary education.

The opportunity to go to college is perhaps the ultimate testament to the American dream, for education is one of the surest returns known this side of the NASDAQ. I know of three guarantees to get ahead in our society. The first is the lottery. If someone wins the Powerball and walks home (heavily guarded) with a cool $100 million, she probably has little to worry about in life, at least financially speaking. The second is marriage. Ours is still a society that offers an immediate pathway to financial and social reward through the marriage clause. Astute readers will quickly note the downside of both these strategies: the odds that either will happen are low, and their propensity to dissolve over time is high.

Education, however, is a true guarantee. Educational capital, once attained, cannot be taken away. Yes, we may loose the precise skills learned in algebra, physics, or language arts, but the processes we derive from taking those courses remain throughout our lives. Disregarding the tongue-in-cheek examples cited previously, achieving a bachelor's degree or higher has the potential to lift people from one social stratum to another and, for individuals from disadvantaged backgrounds, provides a future that is much different from the history they leave behind. Whereas social and cultural capital, as suggested by my colleagues in this volume, provide the foundation for educational attainment, the educational capital gained from a solid education has a reciprocal effect by forever changing the social and cultural dynamics of not only the beneficiaries but also of the people within those individuals' social circle, especially immediate family. Although gaps in who goes to college and who ultimately succeeds remain, it still holds true that education has the greatest potential to benefit all.

As other authors have noted, our difficulty lies in how well we prepare our underserved youth. As Choy and associates note in Chapter Four, almost all students expect to go to college, but not all do. Nineteen of twenty eighth-grade students from lower socioeconomic backgrounds or with parents of subcollege experience expect to go to college, but only two-thirds (or thirteen of twenty) actually do (Gladieux and Swail, 1998). At the other end of the spectrum, as shown by Cabrera and La Nasa (see Chapter Two), almost all students from affluent backgrounds and with educated parents go to college. Chapters One through Five make it clear that access to higher education is more an issue of social and cultural capital than anything else. Those with the tools make use of them, and those without have much fewer options. Thus, lower-SES youth are confronted with a path to obtaining higher education that is somewhat like digging through Alcatraz with a spoon—patience and diminished expectations are the watchwords.

The Reality of School Reform

Since *A Nation at Risk* (1983) was published, educators, policymakers, and researchers have been spinning yarn about what needs to happen within our school systems to overcome the mediocrity reported in the infamous Carnegie report. Empirically, the evidence is clear: we need higher academic standards, a better-prepared cadre of teachers, motivated instructional leaders and the professionalization of teaching, safe school buildings and learning environments, and equal and appropriate access to technology. Readers will quickly note that these represent only a smattering of the critical areas facing education, for the learning process is complex and diverse. And even if they did represent the most critical issues for instilling radical change in our system, we also clearly understand that they represent only the within-school process. Although public education is a significant component of the learning and maturation process, what happens outside of school is where the real learning takes place. What happens during nonschool time is key to the aspirations and motivations of our youth. Reform programs targeting activities taking place out of school are daunting. Their success rests on their ability to change attitudes across the United States with regard to teaching and learning.

There are three realities about educational reform with which we must come to grips. First, without a change in the public attitude toward how we educate our youth and the priority we place on education, no amount of school-based change will evoke the change necessary to level the playing field. During the past three decades, we have begun to more fully understand the importance of community support, parent involvement, and other societal issues on student learning.

The second reality is that school reform, at any level, takes time. Lots of time. Even when we come to terms on key educational issues and strategies, the time between policy development, practical implementation, and a change in student outcomes is long—in many cases, longer than most policymakers are willing to accept. Unfortunately, our state-controlled system of education makes matters worse. To add some perspective, imagine educational change as a series of dominoes waiting to fall. It takes a handful of bold states to take the initial steps that nudge other states, one by one, to start piling onto the bandwagon. Case in point: in 1983, the Carnegie Commission suggested a minimum standard of course requirements for high school graduates: four years of English, three years of mathematics, three years of sciences, three years of social sciences, and two years of foreign language. Sixteen years later, only thirteen states have adopted these minimum standards for graduation, and seven of those achieved this status in the last two years (CCSSO, 1998).

Of course, the discussion to this point assumes that we are able to quantify school reform, which, of course, we cannot. We often treat school reform as a finite process that will be achieved at some point in the future. Our third reality is that educational reform is infinite, a continual renewal of our beliefs and practices. It is a process that can never be completed, and neither should it be. Rather, as our society continues to evolve, so must our educational system. Standards derived to meet today's needs may well be limiting tomorrow. The issues described earlier—teacher preparation, school safety, educational technology—will always be important and evolving issues. We will continue to strive to do better, knowing full well that we are, as in the vernacular of the Beach Boys, on an endless journey.

The problem, as I see it, is that the dichotomy between the good systems and the not-so-good systems—the educational haves and have-nots—presents problems in terms of educational reform. Those schools, communities, and students at the upper end of the educational spectrum make change more quickly and powerfully than others. They have the resources to make the changes and, perhaps more importantly, the political will within the community to ensure that change occurs. Less fortunate school systems have a much more difficult time navigating the waters of change. They are often ill equipped to implement complex policies that bring about dynamic, positive systemic change.

All in all, our free public system of education is unsurpassed in the world. We educate over fifty million students each year, and that number will continue to grow over time. But the sheer magnitude of the system suggests that some students will ultimately fall through the cracks, particularly if these students come from socioeconomically disadvantaged backgrounds. Even if it were a small percentage, say, 1 percent, we would be losing 500,000 students a year. That's too many. But we lose more than 1 percent. We do a pretty good job, on average, with students from middle class and higher upbringings. We do not do nearly as well with less fortunate students. For them, with consideration of all the other barriers along the journey, the educational system is a place rather than a process. It is an end rather than a means. Take the case of college participation rates among low-SES eighth graders. As shown by Cabrera and La Nasa (see Chapter Two) only 144 out of a class of 1,000 eighth graders ended up enrolling in college.

And regardless of how much the system improves, whether we draw a line in the sand ten, twenty, or fifty years down the road, students on the lower end of things will receive less than other, more fortunate students. There is no evidence to suggest that things will change in a capitalist environment where money translates directly into influence and advantage. Education is not an island.

Fingers in the Dike

My point is that the educational system, no matter how well intentioned, will not adequately provide the resources that low-income, underrepresented, high-need students require. The system is just not built to do that. Youth with these background characteristics require the most attention and resources, yet they receive the least.

Programs focused on providing additional or supplementary support services to disadvantaged students can help fill gaps where the system fails. These programs, sometimes emanating from colleges and universities, sometimes from the community, and occasionally from within the school system itself, provide a wide array of services for needy students, including tutoring, mentoring, test-taking skill development, study and time-keeping skills, college awareness, financial planning, and a host of other strategies aimed at making college possible. These programs are, for lack of a better term, the "finger in the dike" component of our educational system. For students of need, they fill the holes where students flow out of the system.

Precollege outreach designed to motivate and prepare students for postsecondary education is part of all schools in some fashion or another. Some would argue that the ideals behind early intervention and college preparation programs are truly at the core of the U.S. school system—preparing students for lifelong learning and college opportunities. But that which takes the form of separate and distinct early intervention and college outreach efforts for some students are often considered normal or average scholastic practice for others.

SAT and ACT preparation, college awareness activities, academic support services—our higher-echelon schools entrench these activities into their core curricula. Other, less fortunate schools struggle to include these important issues as add-ons or rely on outside entities to provide this information to their schools and children. In other words, that which is a de facto facet of some children's education is either entirely missing for others or is included in an ad hoc and often incomplete fashion.

A Brief History

Clearly, there have been and continue to be systematic efforts at raising the level of student preparation and readiness of all students for postsecondary work. The federal TRIO programs are perhaps the most notable of all outreach efforts. Borne of the War on Poverty campaign of the 1960s, Upward Bound, Talent Search, and Student Support Services were established to help provide supplementary academic support to low-income, historically underrepresented students. Later reauthorization of the Higher Education Act of 1965 (HEA) broadened the program to include the McNair program and other, specialized Upward Bound programs. Currently, the TRIO menu now offers services from middle school to graduate level, serving over seventy-five thousand students annually.

More recently, Congress created the Gaining Early Awareness and Readiness for Undergraduate Programs (GEARUP) program as part of the 1998 reauthorization of the Higher Education Act. Although some may argue that GEARUP and TRIO are similar programs, there are a few fundamental differences between the two. The most salient difference is that GEARUP programs must target a cohort of students rather than individual students who meet the criteria for services. Second, the GEARUP statute demands a coordinated web of partnerships between local educational agencies (that is, schools), community partners, and postsecondary institutions. Many TRIO programs do these things as well, but the articulation in federal law mandates this partnership in GEARUP.

And we should not assume that the federal government has been alone in providing programs to help students prepare for college. A number of states have legislated similar efforts. California is perhaps the most notable of the states investing heavily in early intervention programs; it spends about $40 million each year in support of outreach to middle and high school students.

Community groups and not-for-profit organizations also play a role. I Have A Dream™ (IHAD), perhaps the most well-known entity, operates 180 programs around the country. Other networks have been formed to provide support services, such as Advancement Via Individual Determination (AVID) and Mathematics, Engineering, and Science Achievement (MESA). Additionally, local church groups, business groups, and other civic programs, although small, do help students prepare for life beyond high school.

The basic problem lies in the fact that none of these programs is broad enough to provide services to all needy students. For instance, it is estimated that the TRIO programs are able to serve no more than 10 percent of the eligible student population in the United States under current budget provisions. Based on current congressional funding, serving the entire eligible population would require an annual expenditure of over $6 billion. Other programs, such as I Have a Dream, are not structured so that students or schools can just sign up. Rather, students can participate only if they are lucky enough to be in the right district, school, and in some cases, classroom.

Describing the Landscape

The fact is that we really do not know very much about these "finger in the dike" programs. We know about the large, national- and regional-type programs, but we do not know what the universe looks like. A few studies were done in the 1990s to gain some perspective on these programs, but they targeted college-based programs only, neglecting the school- and community-based programs that almost certainly make up a large proportion of the universe (Cahalan and Farris, 1990; Chaney, Lewis, and Farris, 1995).

To provide a more accurate perspective on the outreach phenomena, the College Board, in association with The Education Resources Institute and the Council for Opportunity in Education, conducted the National Survey of Outreach Programs (2000).[1] Conducted during the 1999–2000 school year, the survey sought to provide detailed information about all types of early intervention programs, not just those sponsored by postsecondary institutions. Parallel to the survey was a series of focus groups held around the country with outreach program directors to provide a qualitative texture to the analysis. Together, this information provides a unique perspective on the landscape of programs across the nation. These data are particularly related to the scope of this volume of *New Directions for Institutional Research* because they provide information about what programs are doing, compared with the needs identified by the other authors.

During the course of data collection in summer 1999 and spring 2000, over 1,100 programs, representing all fifty states, the District of Columbia, Puerto Rico, Guam, and Micronesia, responded to the survey. Programs were restricted to those serving underrepresented students at the precollege level, with a minimum of twelve students per calendar year.

As can be seen in Figure 6.1, about one-third of all respondents were TRIO programs (Upward Bound and Talent Search), and the other major federal initiative, GEARUP, accounted for 9 percent of the respondents. Businesses, private organizations, or individuals sponsored about one-fifth of the programs (see Figure 6.2). On average, programs in the survey had been

Figure 6.1. Distribution of Outreach Programs by Program Type

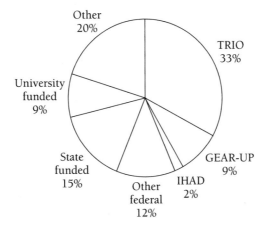

Source: The National Survey of Outreach Programs, The College Board, 2000.

Figure 6.2. Distribution of Outreach Programs by Sponsoring Institution Type

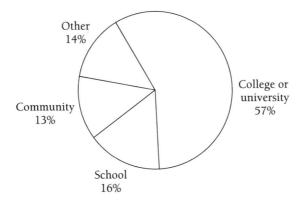

Source: The National Survey of Outreach Programs, The College Board, 2000.

in operation for eleven years. The average age for the TRIO programs was predictably longer (sixteen years) because those programs have had legislative support since the mid-1960s.

More than half of the programs (57 percent) were based at a college or university (see Figure 6.2). This is interesting because the National Center for Education Statistics (NCES) study in 1994–95 found that about one in three colleges had at least one outreach program (NCES, 1996). If our 3:2 ratio of college-based versus non-college-based programs holds true, the nationally weighted NCES sample would suggest that in total about one thousand six hundred fifty outreach programs exist.[2] However, we expect that the NCES studies, as well as the College Board study, are under-representative of the total outreach activities in existence. Therefore, the non–higher education–based programs are of great importance. Of this sector, 37 percent (or 16 percent of the total) were school based, and 30 percent (or 13 percent of the total) were community based. Not surprisingly, most TRIO programs (80 percent) generally operated out of a postsecondary institution, whereas GEARUP programs tended to operate from schools (39 percent) and IHAD programs were largely community based (69 percent). The majority of other federally and non–federally funded programs were based on college campuses.

For nearly one-half (46 percent) of all programs, the primary location of program services was a college campus (see Figure 6.3). For GEARUP programs, however, services were typically delivered at an elementary or secondary school (80 percent). Elementary and secondary schools were also the primary location of services for about one-half of IHAD programs, one-third of TRIO and state-funded programs, and one-fifth of university-funded programs, suggesting that a substantial number of programs had strong ties to K–12 schools and school systems. About one-half of all programs served students of a particular school or school district, and one-fourth targeted a particular community. The majority of TRIO, GEARUP, and IHAD programs targeted services toward students attending a particular school or school district.

About two-thirds (67 percent) of programs were year-round, providing services to students during both the academic year and the summer. Four out of five TRIO, GEARUP, and IHAD programs reported that they were year-round, compared with only one in three university-funded programs. About one-fifth (18 percent) of all programs operated only during the school year, whereas 15 percent operated summer-only programs. About one-half (53 percent) of all programs offered services to students both during school hours and after school, and 60 percent of all programs offered services on the weekends. The duration of program services varied, with some programs offered for a few days and others for several years. Program capacity also varied, averaging 636 students and ranging up to the tens of thousands. About one-half (46 percent) of all programs were capable of serving fewer than one hundred students per year, one-fourth had a capac-

**Figure 6.3. Distribution of Outreach Programs
by Location of Services**

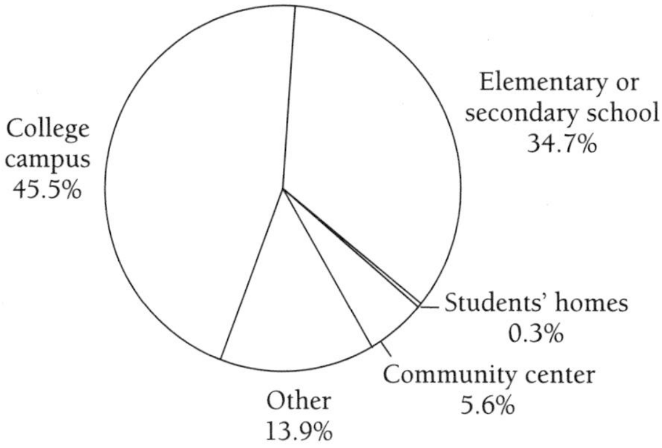

College
campus
45.5%

Elementary or
secondary school
34.7%

Students' homes
0.3%

Community center
5.6%

Other
13.9%

Source: The National Survey of Outreach Programs, The College Board, 2000.

ity between one hundred and five hundred students, and one-fourth had a capacity of more than five hundred students.

Over 90 percent of programs were targeted at students in middle school or beyond, and over 50 percent targeted ninth grade and up (Figure 6.4). This is an interesting but expected finding because most of the literature suggests that these interventions need to start early. One would perhaps have hoped that more programs were targeted at the middle years and earlier. Upon reviewing the academic course-taking patterns of students from the High School and Beyond cohort, U.S. Department of Education policy analyst Cliff Adelman has stated that "colleges should be working more with disadvantaged students while they are still in secondary school, and, if possible, earlier" (1995, p. viii). The GEARUP program, a Department of Education initiative since Adelman's comment, requires programs to start at the seventh-grade level or earlier. As the survey shows, 86 percent of the GEARUP programs did start at the middle school level, and another 8 percent started in elementary school. The remaining GEARUP students were high school students left over from the National Early Intervention Scholarship Program (NEISP) program, the legislative precursor to GEARUP.

What Do These Programs Do?

Previous chapters in this volume have discussed the importance of college awareness and how early exposure to universities facilitates college enrollment. In view of this, it is encouraging to find out that almost 90 percent of the programs responding to this survey focus on college attendance and

**Figure 6.4. Average Starting Point
for Outreach Programs**

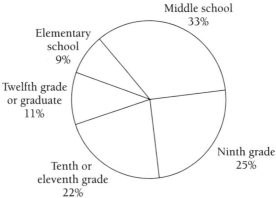

Source: The National Survey of Outreach Programs, The College Board, 2000.

awareness as their primary goals (Figure 6.5). These goals appear to be relatively more common for TRIO and GEARUP programs, likely because both programs were explicitly created to focus on college access.

Building student self-esteem and providing role models were also common goals, reported by 84 percent and 81 percent of respondents, respectively. As Levine and Nidiffer (1996) conclude in their book *Beating the Odds,* support and encouragement from a mentor, whether a parent, relative, or empathetic member of the community, can play a critical role in college enrollment for students from lower-income families. Other goals include increasing college completion, reducing high school dropout rates, improving academic skills, and involving parents.

The particular services offered by programs tell a better story of what they actually do. Figure 6.6 shows that many of the activities focused around college and career awareness, social development, and academic support. The highest-ranked service was college awareness, and a perusal of the list reveals that it included a number of related activities, including campus visits, meetings with faculty and students, and college fairs. Academic support activities focused on a number of areas, from content knowledge (math, science, reading, writing) to skill development (study, test taking, computer, critical thinking).

Program services are delivered via a variety of instructional approaches. About three-fourths of all programs utilized workshops (79 percent) and classroom instruction (75 percent). Role modeling, tutoring, and mentoring were also frequently used by all types of programs but particularly by IHAD programs. More than one-half of all programs also used assessment and test-

Figure 6.5. Goals of Outreach Programs

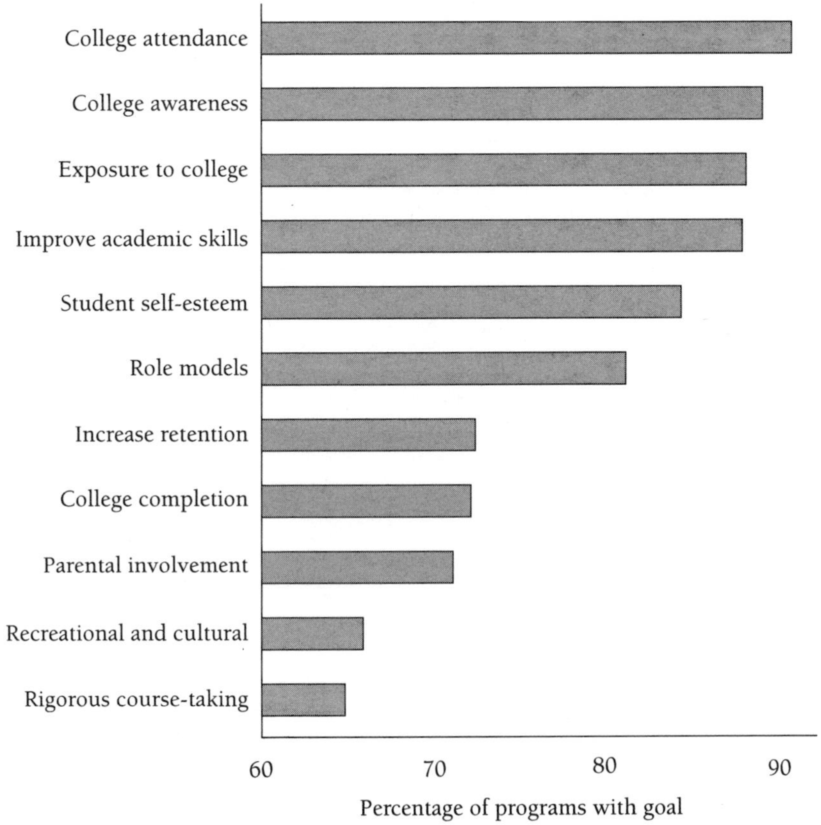

Source: The National Survey of Outreach Programs, The College Board, 2000.

ing practice for their students (60 percent) or peer group learning groups (56 percent), a well-documented approach to academic and social development among underrepresented populations (Fullilove and Treisman, 1990).

By definition, early intervention programs generally focus on helping educationally or economically disadvantaged students aspire to and prepare for higher education. Survey data, as in Figure 6.7, show that the three most targeted student populations included low-income, minority, and first-generation students, representing high areas of most concern for policymakers and educators. Programs also targeted vari ous levels of the education pipeline (middle and high school), students of various academic abilities (both high and low), and also additional student backgrounds (for example, men and women).

Figure 6.6. Services Offered by Outreach Programs (by percentage)

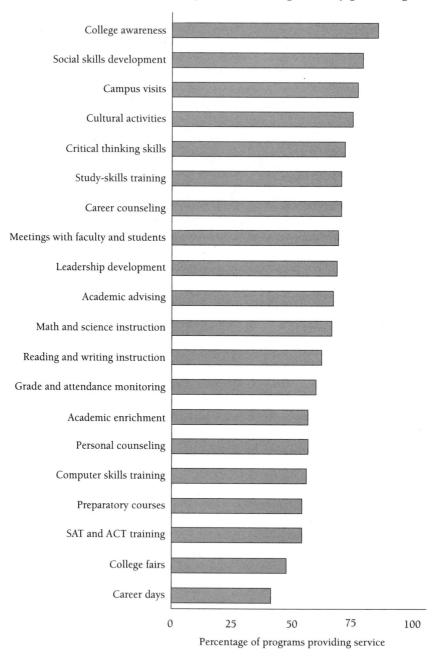

Source: The National Survey of Outreach Programs, The College Board, 2000.

Figure 6.7. Student Groups Targeted by Outreach Programs (by percentage)

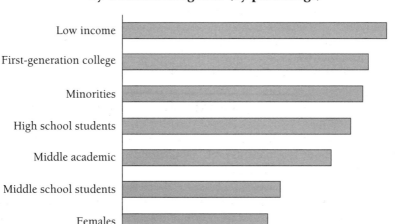

Percentage of programs targeting group

Source: The National Survey of Outreach Programs, The College Board, 2000.

A number of other significant findings came out of the National Survey of Outreach Programs, including the following:

- About half (49 percent) of the responding programs received financial support from the federal government, about one-fourth received financial support from state governments, and one-fourth received financial support from colleges and universities.
- Parental involvement was a common theme that emerged from the focus group discussions. More than two-thirds (69 percent) of all programs offered a parental component, whereas about one-fifth (22 percent) of all programs mandated parental involvement.
- Programs offered a number of rewards for students, including certificates of recognition (69 percent) and scholarships.

- Eighty-seven percent of programs had at least one paid staff member, and the majority of programs employed both full-time and part-time staff. Over half (57 percent) employed college students, but only 10 percent employed high school students. Nearly one-half (43 percent) of all responding programs used volunteers.
- Four out of five programs required an average of seventeen hours of pre-service training for staff members. Over 90 percent of TRIO programs required an average of twenty hours of preservice training.
- Almost all (94 percent) responding programs reported that they conducted program evaluations. About three-fourths (75 percent) reported that they track program completion, and 64 percent reported that they track high school graduation. Only 29 percent of all programs reported tracking graduation from college.

Of great concern is the last list entry regarding program evaluation. Although most programs claim to conduct evaluations, recent studies and reviews find just the opposite (Gandara and Bial, forthcoming; Tierney, forthcoming). Patricia Gandara, in her national search for empirical analysis of precollege outreach programs, has found only a few handfuls of program evaluations that are empirically sound. Others are either poorly done, internally biased, or nonexistent. Remembering that the College Board study was conducted to help describe the landscape of programs, we still are very much in the dark about what works best in programs. With the exception of a few recent studies (most notably the Upward Bound evaluation), most of what we know is anecdotal. For instance, we know that mentoring, tutoring, and role modeling can work, and we know that study skills, academic support, and career awareness are all important. But we also know that not all mentoring programs are the same; some are better and some are worse. In fact, it is entirely plausible that poorly conducted programs may do an injustice to students and have a reverse impact.

What It All Means

As stated at the outset of this chapter, the long-term strategy involves the redefinition of our public-school system. Without large-scale reform, we do not have much chance of changing the direction of mass numbers of lives. I often quote Art Levine and Jana Nidiffer from their book *Beating the Odds* (1996, p.144), where they say that the task of changing lives is "retail not wholesale," or as they also state, that it takes one arm around one child to make a significant impact on students, especially those without many role models to emulate. In fact, when talking with students who recently graduated from college, they were more likely to respond that it took more than one arm around one child. In some cases, it took four or five sets of arms to help get them through the hurdles. The problem with retail-type, one-by-one policy is that it is hard to ramp up any significant programming at a national level that can focus down to the individual level. The federal programs described in this chapter try to do that, but we simply do not have the human, let alone financial, resources to focus on millions of students individually ever year. And that's why we must look to systemic means for solving our long-term challenges.

In the meantime, the outreach programs, described in some detail here, are a helpful crutch for us. Perhaps when we reach the end of time and school reform is complete, none of these programs will exist. However, until that unlikely goal is realized, we need to focus on what these programs should be doing and how they should do it. So, all that said, here are four concrete areas on which we can start working:

1. *Ramping up current outreach activities to reach more of our youth.* It is not enough to serve only a small percentage of our youth through outreach. We need to ensure that each and every young person is offered the opportunity to be involved in an outreach or college preparation program in middle and high school. At the federal level, we need to provide more money to proven programs. TRIO, currently budgeted at approximately $600 million, could easily be doubled or tripled to meet current need. The GEARUP program, although in its infancy, would also benefit from a much larger investment from Congress. Many other nonfederal programs are enjoying rapid expansion, but they are still relatively small and cover only certain geographic territories across the nation.

2. *Improving the instructional quality and delivery of outreach programs.* Providing a service is not necessarily good enough. We must strive to provide quality services to all students in a public school environment, regardless of their school or community's SES. Outreach programs must consider issues of standards of practice to ensure that proven strategies to help students are the norm rather than the exception. For example, although mentoring programs have proven very successful in many communities, several programs have found that appropriate training and careful mentor selection is critical to a positive experience for the student. Unfortunately, too many outreach programs in existence today are not held to any standard of excellence as they serve the young people in our communities. We believe that each of the programs operating in a public school environment must show that they have the tools and expertise to provide the very best service and most current information to the students and families they serve.

3. *Expanding opportunities for networking among programs.* If one asks educators what the single greatest professional development tool is, they will tell you it is the opportunity to network with their colleagues. Unfortunately, staff from different programs almost never have the opportunity to meet and share experiences. In many cases, the programs are considered competitive, thus discouraging communication.

We need to open up these lines of communication and provide more opportunities for programs to interact and work together to help kids.

4. *Linking outreach programs directly to our schools and long-term systemic plans.* We cannot expect outreach programs themselves to have any long-term or systemic impacts on our educational systems unless they have, at their core, a desire to help change the very system whose failure required their existence. Simply put, if outreach programs do not work closely and as a partner with our schools, they will not become part of the long-term solution to our educational woes. In fact, some would argue that they become a distraction from real change in our schools. By communicating and working toward the same goals, schools can partner effectively with programs and receive support from the higher education, business, and community sectors to provide a better education for all students—and plug more of the holes in the dike.

Notes

1. The National Survey of Outreach Programs was directed by Dr. Swail while at the College Board. Further information on the National Survey, including a more elaborate analysis and presentation of data, may be found at http://www.collegeboard.org.

2. The NCES study calculated that 1,100 colleges and universities had at least one outreach program. Thus, a calculation of 3:2 brings 1,650.

References

Adelman, C. *The New College Course Map and Transcript Files.* Washington, D.C.: Office of Educational Research and Improvement, U.S. Department of Education, 1995.

Cahalan, M., and Farris, E. *College Sponsored Tutoring and Mentoring Programs for Disadvantaged Elementary and Secondary Students: A Higher Education Survey Report.* Washington, D.C.: U.S. Department of Education, 1990.

Chaney, B., Lewis, L., and Farris, E. *Programs at Higher Education Institutions for Disadvantaged Precollege Students.* Washington, D.C.: Office of Educational Research and Improvement, U.S. Department of Education, 1995. (NCES 96–230)

College Board. *National Survey of Outreach Programs Directory.* Washington, D.C.: College Board, 2000.

Council of Chief State School Officers. "Key State Education Policies on K–12 Education." *Standards, Graduation, Assessment, Teacher Licensure, Time and Attendance: A 50-State Report.* Washington, D.C.: CCSSO, 1998.

Fullilove, R. E., and Treisman, P. U. "Mathematics Achievement Among African American Undergraduates at the University of California, Berkeley: An Evaluation of the Mathematics Workshop Program." *Journal of Negro Education,* 1990, *59*(3), 463–478.

Gandara, P., and Bial, D. *Paving the Way to Higher Education: K–12 Intervention Programs for Underrepresented Youth.* Washington, D.C.: National Postsecondary Education Cooperative, U.S. Department of Education, forthcoming.

Gladieux, L. E., and Swail, W. S. "Financial Aid is Not Enough: Improving the Odds of College Success." *The College Board Review,* 1998, *185* (Summer), 16–21, 30–31.

Hossler, D., Braxton, J., and Coopersmith, G. "Understanding Student College Choice." In J. C. Smart (ed.), *Higher Education: Handbook of Theory and Research.* Vol. 5. New York: Agathon Press, 1989.

Hossler, D., Schmit, J., and Vesper, N. *Going to College: How Social, Economic, and Educational Factors Influence the Decisions Students Make.* Baltimore: Johns Hopkins University Press, 1999.

Levine, A., and Nidiffer, J. *Beating the Odds: How the Poor Get to College.* San Francisco: Jossey-Bass, 1996.

Myers, D., and Schirm, A. *The Impacts of Upward Bound: Final Report for Phase I of the National Evaluation.* Washington, D.C.: U.S. Department of Education, Planning and Evaluation Services, 1999.

National Center for Education Statistics (NCES). National Educational Longitudinal Study of 1988. Restricted file. Washington, D.C.: National Center for Education Statistics, U.S. Department of Education, 1996. (NCES 96–130)

National Commission on Excellence in Education. *A Nation at Risk: The Imperative for Educational Reform.* Washington, D.C.: U.S. Department of Education, 1983.

Perna, L. W. "Differences in the decision to attend college among African Americans, Hispanics, and Whites." *Journal of Higher Education,* 2000, 71(2), 117–141.

Tierney, W. G. "Cautionary Tales: Evaluation and College Preparation Programs." In W. G. Tierney and L. S. Hagedorn (eds.), *Extending Their Reach: Strategies for Increasing Access to College.* Albany: State University of New York Press, forthcoming.

WATSON SCOTT SWAIL is senior policy analyst for SRI International.

7

This chapter provides useful information regarding the National Educational Longitudinal Study database that was used for many of the studies in this volume. The author provides relevant background and helpful instructions so that others may use this valuable resource from the National Center for Education Statistics.

Using National Educational Longitudinal Study Data to Examine the Transition to College

Lutz Berkner

The National Education Longitudinal Study of 1988 (NELS) is a survey of a nationally representative sample of students who were in the eighth grade in 1988. These students were surveyed again in 1990 (when most of them were in the tenth grade), in 1992 (when most were in their senior year of high school), and in 1994 (two years after most had graduated from high school). The responses to the 1992 and 1994 follow-up surveys provide a rich source of data for research on college access, choice, and persistence during the early years of college. The latest data release cumulates the data from all four years (NCES, 1996a). The NELS 2000 will provide further data on college persistence and degree completion, and these data should be available in 2002.

The 1994 NELS surveyed approximately fourteen thousand respondents who had graduated from high school in 1992, including about nine thousand who had gone on to college. In addition to the usual demographic and socioeconomic background variables, the NELS survey includes a wide variety of questions about students' educational aspirations and plans, college and financial aid applications, concerns about college costs, and sources of information about going to college. The academic background data include high school transcripts, SAT and ACT scores, and scores from cognitive tests developed for NELS that allow for comparisons between those who attended college and those who did not. Additional information is available from surveys of parents and teachers, as well as aggregate data describing the schools these students attended. A good overview of the

NELS surveys ("What Is NELS: 88/2000?") as well as an extensive list of publications that describe the survey methodology or have analyzed the data are available on the National Center for Education Statistics (NCES) Web site at http://www.nces.ed.gov under Surveys>Longitudinal Studies.

The NELS data are available from NCES in two formats: unit record data that can be accessed through an Electronic Codebook System (ECB) and tables of descriptive statistics that can be generated by the Data Analysis System (DAS). The ECB and DAS are Windows-based software developed by NCES. Both can be downloaded for use on a personal computer (PC).

Electronic Codebook Files

The unit record files accessible through the ECB software contain the original items from the student, parent, and teacher questionnaires and interviews; descriptive information about the secondary and postsecondary schools attended; and derived composite variables that categorize course-taking patterns, college enrollment spells, and the socioeconomic status of students. Most of the important variables from the survey are included in the NELS public-use data files, which are available on a compact disc (CD) (NCES, 1996c) through the NCES Web site. A more extensive restricted file is available only to researchers who have applied for a license from NCES (NCES, 1996a).

An older version of the ECB software, which was released in 1996, accompanies the NELS data files on the CD. Updated software is available from NCES on a separate CD, *Electronic Codebooks for Windows 95/98* (NCES, 2000). Although the latter CD contains no data, it has better instructions about the ECB and may be used with the previously released NELS data files.

The ECB contains a list of all variables in the NELS files, organized by sections according to the survey year and type of respondent (student, parent, teacher) or source (transcripts, schools). The section name appears at the top of the screen, and the system used to name the variables usually makes it easy to identify the survey year and type of respondent. By highlighting a variable of interest on the list (categorical variables appear in green; continuous, in blue; and verbatim strings, in red) and choosing View>Description, one can view either a description of the variable (including the item wording) or the unweighted frequencies. To create a subset of the data for a research project, select or "tag" the variables of interest by checking the box next to the variable name in the ECB list. Then go to File>Output to create two text files for the project. By selecting Output>Codebook Text, the descriptions and frequencies of the selected variables will be output into a text file that can be printed for easy reference and will serve as the codebook for the project. Then choose either Output>SAS-PC or >SPSS to create a text file that contains the programming code to make either an SAS or SPSS data file. The program that is output contains all of the code for assigning labels to variables and categorical values. After some minor editing of the code to designate the correct file locations on your PC, the program can be run to create either an SAS or SPSS data set of the variables for the project.

Although this is a tantalizing treasure trove of data, there are some limitations and many potential pitfalls in using the raw data in these unit record files. Perhaps the greatest of these come from failing to use the appropriate weights (or any weights at all) and from improperly calculating standard errors for statistical tests of significance. These issues are discussed in "Frequently Asked Questions Regarding NELS" on the NCES Web site. NELS is based on a complex sampling design, and certain subgroups are either deliberately overrepresented (such as Asians, Hispanics, and private schools) or underrepresented because of low response rates (such as high school dropouts). Research results based on unweighted numbers will not accurately reflect the actual distributions in the population of students being studied.

In order to make the eighth-grade sample representative of tenth graders in 1990 and twelfth graders in 1992, the sample was freshened by adding new members in 1990 and 1992. Moreover, the 1994 survey was based only on a subsample of approximately 14,000 cases from the 1992 respondents. Comparisons based on unweighted counts in separate years were considered invalid. An analysis of student behavior or attitudes over time requires using the appropriate panel weight so that the same cases are represented in each year. However, the choice of weights may result in quite different results. For example, if the panel weight for all eighth graders who were also in the 1994 sample is used, one finds that 63 percent went on to college; however, if the panel weight for those who were 1992 high school graduates is used, one finds that 75 percent went on to college. Multivariate analysis of the data without the proper weights is also inappropriate. Moreover, the calculation of standard errors in the standard SPSS and SAS programs does not correct for the survey design effects and may result in misinterpreting the tests of significance.

It is also important to understand the structure of the unit record data files and how the various units are linked. In general, the student respondent is the unit of analysis. The aggregate data describing the secondary schools attended are linked to individual student records. The data may be used to analyze the relationship between school characteristics and student behavior; however, it is not appropriate to use the data to study schools. Similarly, the teachers in the study represent the teachers of the students in the sample, and they may not be representative of all teachers in the survey year.

The data files on the CD primarily contain the raw data from the NELS surveys through 1994, which were released a few years later. Any new composite variables developed for NCES publications after 1996 will not be found on this CD. These include the academic qualification index and its components, the college pipeline variables, and several new weights. NCES releases new composite variables by updating the online DAS files described in the following section. In addition to the ECB for the raw data available only on a CD, there is a second ECB that includes only the variables in the DAS (including all updates since 1996). The ECB for the DAS variables can be downloaded from the DAS Web site noted in the following section by selecting Download DAS Application>Download ECB. The unit record data for the variables in this ECB are available only to those with NCES licenses. Nevertheless, the variables are available for research through the DAS.

The Data Analysis System

The DAS is a software application that allows users to specify and generate their own tables of descriptive statistics (percentages, means, and medians) from the NELS data. It does not allow access to individual-level unit record data. The tables produced by the DAS are based on weighted numbers and include the appropriate standard errors adjusted for survey design effects. The DAS will also produce a matrix of correlation coefficients that can be used by SPSS for some types of multivariate analysis.

The DAS software, survey data files, and documentation are available on the NCES DAS Web site (http://www.nces.ed.gov/das). The Web site includes a Help file and general instructions about using the software, which requires no knowledge of programming. A convenient feature of this Web site is that it contains a complete list of the variables in the data file and a complete codebook with variable descriptions and weighted frequencies that can be downloaded as Zipped-text files. To find the variable list and codebook, select the DAS Update button and scroll down to the NELS survey. (The frequencies in the DAS are weighted; the Electronic Codebook for the DAS variables discussed earlier shows unweighted frequencies. The variable descriptions are identical in both.)

The DAS data file contains about one thousand variables, including many of the items from the original surveys (that is, the raw data in the 1994 Electronic Codebook) and all new composite variables created for NCES reports published after 1996. The DAS data files on the Web site are continually updated, and the Web site includes a list of all recently added variables. The NELS 1988–1994 DAS (NCES, 1996b) contains most items from the surveys that are particularly relevant to research on college access and choice.

Instructions for using the DAS and downloading the software are found on the NCES DAS Web site by selecting Download DAS Application. The front end of the DAS software is similar to the ECB. The user is presented with a list of variables and can view the descriptions and the frequencies for each variable. Unlike the ECB, the frequencies in the DAS are weighted, and the appropriate weight for the particular analysis must be indicated. The user selects a set of row variables and may specify cut points for continuous variables or lump existing values for discrete variables into new categories.

The user then selects column variables for tables. These may be percentage distributions of categorical variables (or of defined ranges of continuous variables), means, medians, or percentage of positive cases. These table parameter files can easily be submitted for processing on the DAS Web site, and results are usually returned in less than an hour.

The DAS variable list and codebook provide the best introduction to and overview of the NELS data that relate to the transition from high school to college. A considerable amount of research and analysis can be done through the DAS, which provides weighted results and appropriately calculated standard errors while avoiding many of the potential pitfalls in working with raw unit record data.

References

National Center for Education Statistics (NCES). National Educational Longitudinal Study of 1988. Restricted file. Washington, D.C.: National Center for Education Statistics, U.S. Department of Education, 1996a. (NCES 96–130)

National Center for Education Statistics (NCES). National Educational Longitudinal Study of 1988, Data Analysis System. Washington D.C.: Office of Educational Research and Improvement, U.S. Department of Education, 1996b. (NCES 96–127)

National Center for Education Statistics (NCES). National Educational Longitudinal Study: 1988–1994, Data Files and Electronic Codebook System. Public use. Washington, D.C.: Office of Educational Research and Improvement, U.S. Department of Education, 1996c. (NCES 96–128)

National Center for Education Statistics (NCES). *Electronic Codebooks for Windows 95/98.* Washington, D.C.: Office of Educational Research and Improvement, U.S. Department of Education, 2000. (NCES 2000–93)

LUTZ BERKNER is a researcher with MPR Associates.

INDEX

Note: Letters in italics refer to figures and tables.

Back Issue/Subscription Order Form

Copy or detach and send to:
Jossey-Bass Publishers, 350 Sansome Street, San Francisco CA 94104-1342
Call or fax toll free!
Phone 888-378-2537 6AM-5PM PST; Fax 800-605-2665

Back issues: Please send me the following issues at $23 each:
(Important: please include series initials and issue number, such as IR90)

1. IR _____

_____

_____

$ _____ Total for single issues

$ _____ Shipping charges (for single issues *only;* subscriptions are exempt
from shipping charges): Up to $30, add $5^{50} • $30^{01}–$50, add $6^{50}
$50^{01}–$75, add $8 • $75^{01}–$100, add $10, $100^{01}–$150, add $12
Over $150, call for shipping charge

Subscriptions   Please ❏ start   ❏ renew my subscription to *New Directions for*
Institutional Research for the year _____ at the following rate:

U.S.	❏ Individual $56	❏ Institutional $99
Canada:	❏ Individual $81	❏ Institutional $124
All Others:	❏ Individual $86	❏ Institutional $129

NOTE: Subscriptions are quarterly, and are for the calendar year only.
Subscriptions begin with the Spring issue of the year indicated above.

$ _____ Total single issues and subscriptions (Add appropriate sales tax
for your state for single issue orders. No sales tax for U.S. subscriptions.
Canadian residents, add GST for subscriptions and single issues.)

❏ Payment enclosed (U.S. check or money order only)

❏ VISA, MC, AmEx, Discover Card #_____ Exp. date_____

Signature _____ Day phone _____

❏ Bill me (U.S. institutional orders only. Purchase order required)

Purchase order #_____

Federal Tax ID 135593032   GST 89102-8052

Name _____

Address _____

_____

Phone_____ E-mail _____

For more information about Jossey-Bass Publishers, visit our Web site at:
www.josseybass.com   **PRIORITY CODE = ND1**

OTHER TITLES AVAILABLE IN THE
NEW DIRECTIONS FOR INSTITUTIONAL RESEARCH SERIES
J. Fredericks Volkwein, Editor-in-Chief